BASIC
POOL

··

ALSO BY BABE CRANFIELD AND LAURENCE S. MOY

The Straight Pool Bible

BASIC
POOL

··

The Ultimate Beginner's Guide

··

Arthur "Babe" Cranfield
and Laurence S. Moy

Skyhorse Publishing

Skyhorse Publishing books may be purchased in bulk at special discounts for sales promotion, corporate gifts, fund-raising, or educational purposes. Special editions can also be created to specifications. For details, contact the Special Sales Department, Skyhorse Publishing, 307 West 36th Street, 11th Floor, New York, NY 10018 or info@skyhorsepublishing.com.

www.skyhorsepublishing.com

10 9 8 7 6 5 4 3 2 1

Library of Congress Cataloging-in-Publication Data is available on file.
ISBN: 978-1-61608-179-9

Printed in China

*D*edicated
to the memories
of Arthur Cranfield, Sr.,
and Mary Moy

Table of Contents

Introduction

Anyone can learn to play pool well. Many have started out with limited natural talent, but nonetheless developed into solid players. Pool is beautiful and democratic in that way. Anyone can apply his or her strengths to the game and excel since the game requires so many different types of skills. There is room in billiards and pool for those blessed with excellent hand-eye coordination, those with very little coordination but strong intellect, those who are systematic but not creative, and those who are creative but not systematic.

Yet some people have dropped the game because it is more difficult than many other pastimes, or struggled for years to reach an enjoyable level of proficiency. Even experienced pool players can at times become dizzy and frustrated with facets of the game. No knowledgeable person would deny that there is a great deal to learn about pool, potentially more than anyone could learn in a lifetime.

That being the case, how can a beginning player get a good start learning the game? Why do some players progress much more quickly than others? How can experienced players rely on coming up with their best play when it counts—under the pressure of competition?

Part of the answer to all of these questions is distilling the many elements of playing pool to their essentials. If you have ever picked up more than one or two books on pool, you've been subjected to excruciating detail on particular shots that you may, or may never, confront in a game. Since so many different possibilities can present themselves on the table, it *is* tempting to teach pool by trying to explain the game one shot at a time. The problem with that approach, however, is that the different types of shots and the different possibilities for how the balls can arrange themselves on the table are limitless.

While no book can teach you everything you need to know to become a good pool player, the chapters that follow approach pool with the goal of sharing concepts that you can use to create your own solutions when you step up to a table. These concepts—which address both the physical and the mental aspects of playing pool well—are presented in a fashion that allows a player to absorb these critical elements easily, and to be able to call upon them during the pressure of a game. By applying the following strategies for attacking the table, you will be able to adapt general principles of correct play to specific situations as they come up.

Playing *correctly* is the key, not how many balls you are able to run off the table in a row. I have taught many players, and have always told them that it is better to run five balls the right way than twenty-five the wrong way. If you learn to run five balls the right way, you'll eventually run twenty-five. The success I have enjoyed at billiards—starting with a junior championship and working my way up to the World Professional Championship in 1964—speaks to the fact that if you learn to play correctly, long runs of the table will follow.

Whether your next game will be a tournament match or part of a night out with a group of friends is up to you. I hope that this book will help you to succeed at pool no matter what the context, which will lead to more enjoyment and, in turn, even greater success. Let's look at the most critical elements in the game of pocket billiards: the essentials of playing pool.

Babe Cranfield

BASIC
POOL

....

Getting Started

As with any other demanding game, your rewards in pool will increase as you improve. As you become more accomplished, the game has an uncanny way of revealing its possibilities and nuances. In pool, perfect execution is not enough. You must be constantly striving to gain knowledge, and you must develop the ability to create solutions to problems that you have never seen before. All of this can make the game seem overwhelmingly daunting and difficult. Those same qualities, however, make pool interesting at all levels of play. There will always be new ways for you to develop as a pool player. The game is rich in its intricacy, variety, and challenges; it is a true lifetime endeavor, impossible to outgrow.

Today, pool is being played in a wide variety of settings: in poolroom leagues, in team competitions, in bar leagues, in weekend tournaments, in clubs, in homes, and in commercial poolrooms. No matter which of these settings you prefer, if you want to improve at pool, you will need to find a place—and the time—to practice on your own. You will never get much better at pool if you only play games and never practice, since you will be depriving yourself of the chance to experiment with different approaches. Once you reach a certain level, it will become absolutely necessary for you to compete against others, in addition to practicing alone, in order to continue to improve. In an ideal world, you would have the time and the money to practice on your own, play against other players, and receive personal instruction.

Even if this is not possible, you can become accomplished at pool if you are willing to practice it seriously as a sport. Take the approach of trying to absorb every bit of information that comes your way during your practice sessions and games. Most of what you learn through both practice and competition is picked up through observation.

Becoming proficient at pool also means recognizing that you can, and should, learn from virtually everyone—even players whom you usually beat. Players who are generally weaker than you may still be superior at some aspect of the game. Don't be so proud that you cheat yourself out of an opportunity to gain more knowledge. By learning how to address more and more situations on the table, you will be building what I call your pool "vocabulary." Increasing this vocabulary will help you every time you step up to the table.

Pool knowledge finds its way to those who are most receptive to it. Those who have not trained themselves to take in all the information that they can are cursed with the fate of repeating their mistakes at the table.

As with learning a new language, improving quickly at pool requires the willingness to risk looking foolish. One of the biggest, and most common, mistakes made in poolrooms everywhere is that of a player who practices only those parts of the game that he or she has already mastered. At some level, it *is* more fun to play, over and over again, those shots that you know you will usually make. No one likes to miss shots, especially if someone else might be watching.

The quickest way to become a better pool player, however, is to start with those parts of your game that make you the *least* comfortable. If you are self-conscious, practice during a time of day when you can enjoy some measure of solitude, or at least, relative quiet. If others happen to be in the room during the time you have set aside to practice, play on a table as far away from the other patrons as possible.

Once you're ready to practice, start by considering what types of shots give you the most trouble, and devote just five to ten minutes to each of these "problem" shots. After isolating your trouble areas and putting in just a little concentrated effort of this type, you will find yourself becoming more comfortable with shots that you once feared.

Your rewards will not be long in coming. The next time you are playing a game and one of those former problem shots comes up, you will be more confident and prepared, and will have more fun with your new, more well-rounded game. You will start to win games against players who used to have the edge over you. You will not repeatedly miss shots that you know you can make.

• The Basics •

Anyone can learn to play pool at an enjoyable level. So let's begin by taking a look at the table and the most basic terms and concepts that apply to the different varieties of pool games. All pool games involve use of a white ball, the cue ball, which is used to knock the numbered balls (called "object balls") into the table pockets. In all of the major pool games, the cue ball is the only ball struck by the cue stick on a legal shot.

A full set of pocket billiard balls consists of a cue ball and fifteen object balls. The colors of the object balls are standardized: the one ball is always yellow, the nine ball is yellow-striped; the two ball is blue, the ten ball is blue-striped; the three ball is red, the eleven ball is red-striped, and so on. Not all games use all fifteen object balls. The most popular game in the United States today is nine-ball, which uses only the object balls numbered one through nine. (Snooker, a billiards game that enjoys massive popularity worldwide, employs different balls, cues, rules, and tables than pool. Given all of these differences, snooker will not be addressed in this book.)

The Table

All pool tables are covered with cloth which is commonly, but mistakenly, called felt. Billiard cloth is one of the most important pieces of equipment needed to play pool properly. Unlike felt, billiard cloth is precisely woven from wool or wool and synthetic threads. Although the color of the cloth used to always be green or blue, the colors have multiplied to accommodate the taste and decor of the many people who select tables for homes or commercial poolrooms.

Pool tables also come in a variety of sizes. The nine-foot table (also known as the "4½ × 9") is the standard size found in most poolrooms and used for most professional tournament play. The playing field on a nine-foot table is 50 by 100 inches. A popular home table size is the 4' × 8' table, since many homes lack a room large enough for a nine-foot table. The pool tables found in most bars are a space-saving 3½′ × 7′. Tournaments and leagues are often played on these as well. (*Any* table requires nearly five feet of space around its perimeter since a full-size cue is 57 or 58 inches long. Thus, a nine-foot table must be placed in a space measuring at least fourteen by eighteen feet.)

Illustration 1 depicts a pool table and its parts. You should become familiar with this terminology, which is used to describe the rules of the different games as well as playing techniques. The end of the table where the balls are racked at the beginning of a game is called the "foot" of the table. The other end is the "head" of the table. Midway across the table's width, and a quarter of a table length from each table end, are two spots: the foot spot and the head spot. These spots are used to mark where balls should be racked and as reference points for other purposes. The base of the top ball in the rack of any pool game should rest exactly on the foot spot.

You'll notice that little circles or diamond-shaped inlays outline the perimeter of the table. These markings are appropriately named "diamonds," and one of their purposes is to delineate parts of the table. Thus, the line formed by connecting the second diamond from the head of each side of the table creates an imaginary line called the "head string." The head string runs exactly over the head spot and, in certain games, the incoming player must take his or her shot from behind the head string if his or her opponent has just "scratched" (pocketed the cue ball).

Basic Rules

Most pool games start by racking the object balls at the foot spot. Each shot begins with a player stroking the cue ball. Each player's turn at the table is called an "inning." In an inning, a player continues until (a) the player fails to pocket a ball; (b) the player completes a "safety" or a "safe"—where the player executes a legal shot (which may or may not involve pocketing a ball) designed to deprive his or her opponent of a shot; (c) the player "fouls" or "scratches"; that is, the player pockets the cue ball, fails to execute a legal shot, or fouls in some other manner; or (d) the player wins the

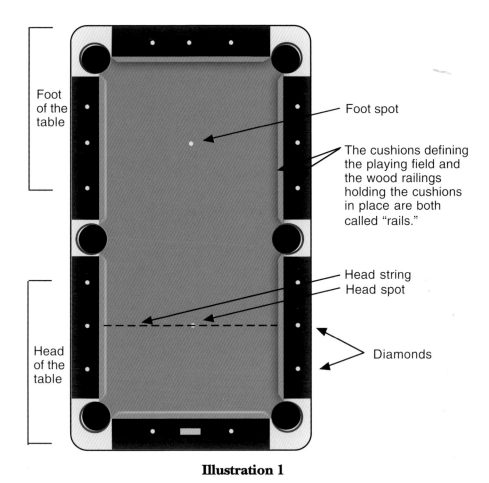

Foot of the table

Foot spot

The cushions defining the playing field and the wood railings holding the cushions in place are both called "rails."

Head string

Head spot

Diamonds

Head of the table

Illustration 1

game. Thus, innings can be as brief as a single shot or can be comprised of a series of shots (a "run").

The most common fouls are pocketing the cue ball or failing to execute a legal shot. In the game of straight pool, for example, the cue ball must touch an object ball, and then either an object ball must be pocketed, or the cue ball or an object ball must touch a cushion. Failure to do so is a foul. There are other fouls, such as touching any of the balls on the table in any way (with your hand, clothing or anything else), touching the cue ball with any part of the cue stick other than the tip, shooting while any of the balls on the table surface are still rolling or spinning, jumping the cue ball out of the playing area, failing to keep at least one foot touching the floor while shooting, double-hitting the cue ball with the cue tip, pushing the cue ball with the cue tip, and illegally jumping the cue ball by dragging under it and lifting it with the cue.

Some games are "call" shot games, where you only get credit for pocketing a shot if you first correctly identify the number of the ball you intend to pocket and the pocket in which you intend to sink the shot. Except in movies and heated gambling matches, no one is obnoxious enough to call *every* shot in a called shot game. That is because most shots are obvious. Sometimes your intended shot is not obvious, however, because you're shooting the cue ball into an area of the table where multiple potential targets lie, or because you intend to "bank" a ball (bounce it off a cushion) into a pocket away from the initial direction of the object ball. In those instances, pool etiquette (an oxymoron to some) dictates that you audibly call your intended object ball and the intended pocket. An example of this would be "six ball in the corner pocket." For a bank, you might say, "two ball, cross-side" or simply, "bank the two ball into the side."

Etiquette

There is much more to pool etiquette. There exists a basic code for proper conduct during a pool match (other than the purely social kind). When it's your inning at the table, you need not rush, but don't stall, either. Pool is a game of rhythm. Winning through stalling your opponent into unconsciousness is a hollow victory.

Basic pool etiquette also requires that you don't do anything to disturb your opponent's concentration. Stay quiet. When your opponent is preparing to shoot, don't move, especially when you're in your opponent's line of sight. Never hover over the table while it's your opponent's inning. If your opponent executes a nice shot or safety, you can show your appreciation by tapping the rubber bumper at the base of your cue against the floor, or simply by saying "nice shot."

Pool etiquette extends even to the chalking of the cue stick. Don't grab the chalk from the rails at the end of your inning. That's just the time when your opponent will need the chalk since the time to chalk is properly just *before* each shot. Obviously, you should not take chalk from the table in the middle of your opponent's inning. After you're done using the chalk, place it face up on the rail so it doesn't make a mess of the table (or your opponent's hands or clothes). The rules of the game also prohibit using strategic placement of the chalk to assist you in aiming or mapping out your shots. Use the diamonds, pockets, or object balls instead.

Both the rules and etiquette require that you rack the object balls "tightly." Although the number of balls racked and the shape of the rack may vary in any game you play, it is critical that you rack the balls tightly. Each of the object balls should be touching its neighbors. A tight rack is needed to make sure that when the rack is touched (or "broken," as it is called—even when the "break" is a gentle stroke that barely disturbs the balls), the object balls behave as they should. Even a barely visible gap between balls in a rack will profoundly affect the break.

Racking the balls tightly when you practice helps you to learn the correct way to play. Racking the balls tightly for your opponent in a game is a basic requirement of good sportsmanship. You should also inspect the rack before you break. Insist upon a tight rack from your opponent, and expect your opponent to become upset with you if you fail to rack the object balls tightly and on the foot spot.

• The Essentials •

1. **Practice in a setting where you will feel comfortable and not self-conscious. Do not fear making mistakes or experimenting.**

2. **Make a point of trying to learn from all players, including less skilled players.**

3. **Learn the names of the different parts of a table and the basic terms of the game. As with any new pursuit, you'll need to understand the language in order to learn the rules and more advanced concepts.**

4. **Observe basic courtesy each time you play a game.**

Equipment Makes a Difference

• "Table in the Back?"—How to Select a Table in a Commercial Poolroom •

Other than picking a table with enough privacy to allow for uninhibited practice, what should be considered when the girl or guy behind the desk asks you what table you want? First off, don't select the same table on each visit. Pool is a game of touch. Subtle factors—the type of cloth on the bed of the table, the resiliency of the cushions, lighting, even acoustics—can play a part in how well you perform. If you constantly play on the same table you will never learn to make the fine adjustments that all good players make when faced with varying conditions.

Although professional players enjoy the most opportunities to play under ideal conditions, it is arguably more important for less advanced players to have the chance to play without the distraction of flawed conditions—tables that lean towards one side or the other, uneven cloth that causes the balls to roll off a straight line, or lighting that throws shadows over the playing field. For the player starting out, it is critical that he or she has the chance to develop a feel for how a table should properly play and how the balls should properly roll.

Take notice of the lighting. Sometimes certain tables have more light fixtures (or, in rooms that are not kept up too well, more working light bulbs) than other tables. In the daytime, you may also want to avoid tables near windows or glass doors, because depending on which direction you are facing when you are trying to line up your shots, glare may impair your vision.

Most poolrooms are laid out with the same types of tables throughout the room. Once in a while, however, you'll encounter a poolroom that has mix-and-match pool tables. Either way, you might as well ask which tables play the best. If you are forced to rely solely on your own judgment in this regard, take the cue ball and hit a few shots on the different tables. This will not take very long since you will be checking mainly for whether the balls will roll in a straight line. This is best done by shooting the cue ball into the pockets from all different angles but always at a very slow speed. Take note of whether the cue ball veers off course towards either the left or the right.

Another big factor to consider when you are picking out your table is the cloth. Avoid cloth that is extremely worn, which will make the balls roll further than expected (i.e., the table will play "fast") in some instances, and create the opposite effect (play "slow") in others. Cloth that is worn out is also more prone to cause "rolls"; that is, areas on the table where the balls will not travel in a straight line. Also, if the cloth is worn, it is quite common that certain parts of the table will have developed tracks or ruts where the cue ball may tend to get stuck along a particular path, especially along the rails. (Another area of the table where tracks develop is from the most popular starting points for breaking the balls towards where the balls are racked.)

Once you have selected your table, however, do not become preoccupied with its idiosyncrasies. Be aware of how the table tends to play so that you can make adjustments, but recognize that all tables have their quirks. All in all, the table will tend to play more perfectly than you will.

• What to Look for in a Pool Cue •

Pool cues range from the inexpensive and purely functional cues found in commercial poolrooms, known as house cues, to ornate, handcrafted custom instruments. For a diagram labeling the various parts of a cue, see illustration 2.

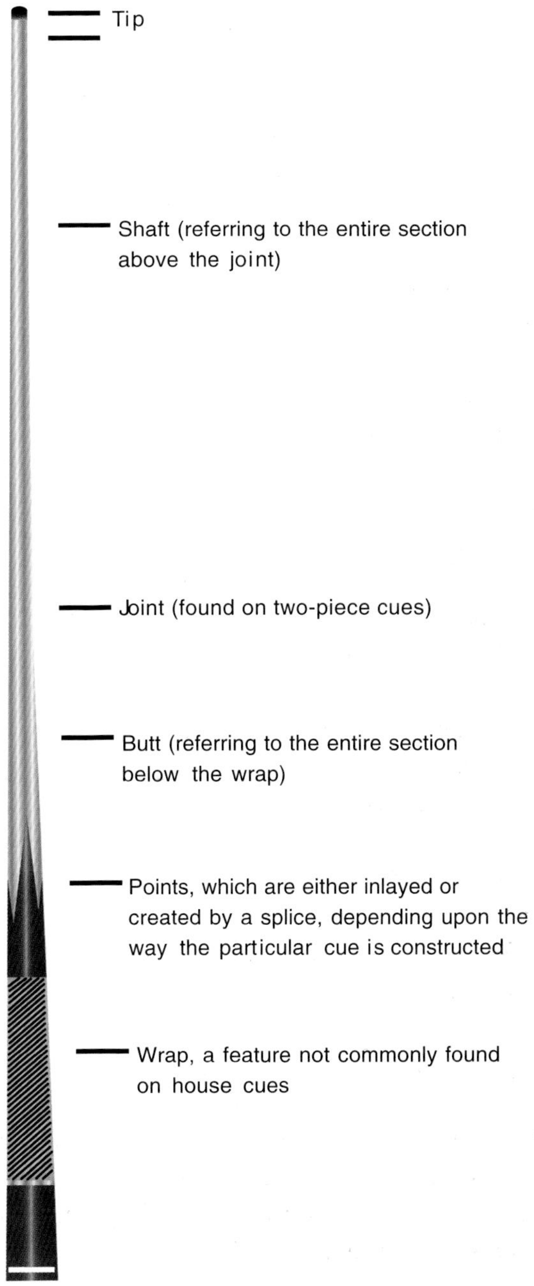

Tip

Shaft (referring to the entire section
above the joint)

Joint (found on two-piece cues)

Butt (referring to the entire section
below the wrap)

Points, which are either inlayed or
created by a splice, depending upon the
way the particular cue is constructed

Wrap, a feature not commonly found
on house cues

Illustration 2

House Cues

On the first few occasions that people play pool, it is usually with one of the one-piece "house" cues supplied by a poolroom. Most house cues are one-piece cues. A good player can play well with a house cue, provided that it has a good tip and is straight. The tip of a cue is the single most important component, although it may also be the least expensive part of the cue. Avoid slip-on and screw-on tips, which are often found on the most cheaply constructed cues. If you are playing with a house cue, you will not have any choice as to what type of leather is used to make the tip, but you can choose a cue with a properly shaped tip.

The tip should be shaped such that the sides of the tip are flush with the sides of the ferrule (the white portion of the cue that is just below the tip and connects the wood of the shaft of the cue to the tip). In addition, the top of the tip should be curved evenly all around, roughly approximate to the curvature of a nickel (illustration 3). The tip of the first cue in illustration 3, cue A, looks just right. The sides of the tip are flush with the sides of the ferrule, and the tip is nicely shaped. The tip on cue B, however, is not shaped at all. A tip this flat will cause you to glance off the cue ball (miscue) whenever you try to aim anywhere other than the center of the cue ball. The tip on cue C has the opposite problem. Here, the tip is shaped too high. Whoever put the tip on cue D never trimmed the tip, and the edges of the tip are not flush with the edges of the ferrule. The cue labeled E has a tip that is too small, and so the tip, once again, is not flush with the ferrule.

Another quality to look for in a tip is the proper hardness. In general, professional and other accomplished players prefer tips on the hard end of the scale. While some pros may prefer a tip slightly less hard than others, any player of that caliber will be using a tip that is firmer than the tips you will typically find on house cues. It's important for the tip to retain its shape so that you can count on it to contact the cue ball in the same way from shot to shot and from game to game. Tips that are too soft do not retain their shape enough to provide this kind of consistency.

Examine the tip of the cue you're planning on using. If you see tiny threads or shredding, the tip is too soft. Try pressing your

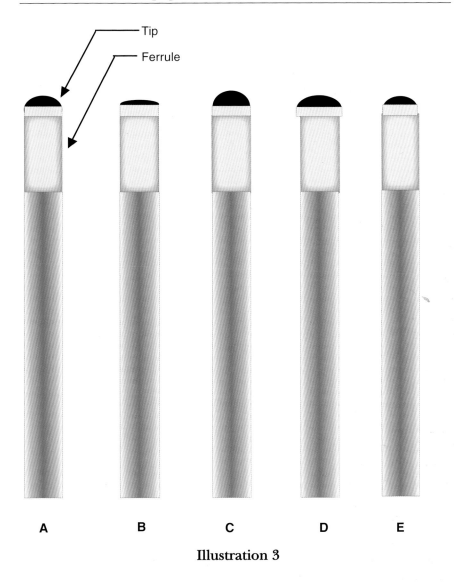

Illustration 3

fingernail into the top and edges of the tip. You should feel little or no "give." Many times, a flat tip indicates that the leather is too soft.

After checking the tip of a cue, check for straightness. This is done by sighting the cue from the back end (the "butt") down towards the tip of the cue, as if you are looking down the barrel of a rifle. As you are looking down the length of the cue, rotate it to check for a possible warp in each direction. Next, roll the cue across the bed of the pool table to see if the cue rolls straight and evenly, or if the cue shimmies as it is rolled.

House cues are marked with the weight in ounces towards the back end of the cues. The weight of the cue you choose to use is more a matter of personal preference than anything else. Most players prefer a cue somewhere in the range of eighteen to twenty-one ounces.

Today, players tend to favor cues on the lighter end of that range since the tables and balls today play fast as compared to the conditions twenty or more years ago. On a slow table, a heavier cue will help to move the balls without an excessively hard stroke.

The weight of house cues is measured in half-ounce increments. If you're starting out and using a house cue, first try a cue weighing eighteen to nineteen ounces, at least until you develop your own preference. Playing with a house cue is a sensible way to introduce yourself to the game. There's no point in investing in a personal pool cue if you're unsure whether you will be playing regularly. Use the above pointers to pick out the most suitable house cue you can find, and then focus on the game instead of the cue. A well-maintained house cue is more than adequate at the beginning stages of the game, and, in fact, superior to some two-piece cues.

Your First Cue

Anyone with more than a casual interest in pool should consider buying their own personal cue stick. The most important advice for buying a personal cue is that you buy something that feels comfortable to you, and that you use that same cue each and every time you play. It is impossible to play pool well without developing a refined sense of touch. Using the same cue every time you play helps you develop that touch. While you may be able to play well with a house cue, buying your own cue will allow you to enjoy consistency in terms of weight, feel, and balance—each time you play.

Personal cues are generally two-piece in design for easier storage and transport. Aside from that common feature, cues vary widely in the way they perform. Before buying your own cue, try as many different types of cues as you can so that you can match your own preferences to the playing qualities and dimensions of the cue.

One difference between a house cue and a more expensive model is that house cues are not necessarily known for being well-balanced. A lot of the weight in a house cue will tend to be towards the butt of the cue. This will make a 20-ounce house cue feel a lot heavier than a custom 20-ounce cue, since most of the weight will be in your back hand, which supports most of the weight of your cue. Once you get a feel for what you like in terms of cue balance, you can gauge it by taking a cue you like and locating the balance point of that cue. Simply hold the cue horizontally and test where on the length of the cue you can place your finger so that the cue balances. Where your finger ends up is the balance point.

Cues other than house cues are usually covered with some type of wrap material (typically linen, leather, or nylon) on the back end. You will develop your own preference for wrap material, but most of the better cues will not use nylon on the wrap, since linen or leather (or no wrap at all) will provide a grip superior to nylon, which can get slippery. On cues with a wrap, the balance point will tend to be about two inches above the wrap.

Most cues are made of wood, but others are made of aluminum, fiberglass, or composites. Avoid all metal cues, which cannot be repaired when they dent. The most traditional material for cues is wood, and you may want to stick with wood until you have a chance to try other types and figure out for yourself whether you prefer some of the less traditional materials.

When shopping for a cue of your own, you will also need to decide on what material you want for the joint of the stick. The choices include metal (stainless steel is the most common metal used today), plastic, or a wood-to-wood connection. Each of these types of joints has its own characteristics and you should play with cues that have joints made from each before you buy. There is no right answer when it comes to a joint for your cue. Buy what feels best.

If you don't know where to start, you will probably be fine with a two-piece cue fifty-eight inches in length (which is the standard length today, up from fifty-seven inches years ago) that weighs about nineteen ounces. Although you will eventually develop a preference concerning how thin or thick the shaft of your cue should be, you can start out with the standard tip and shaft diameter of thirteen millimeters. For beginning players, the joint material and the hardness of the tip will not be big factors. Just make sure your first cue is straight with a properly shaped tip!

For someone relatively new to the game, a modestly priced cue is more than adequate. A beginning player with a relatively inexpensive cue enjoys the same benefit as the owner of a custom model in terms of being able to enjoy the luxury of using the same cue on every occasion. This is more important than anything else when it comes to pool cues.

Given the number of quality manufacturers today (and the pressure from the competition among these producers to provide good quality cues at affordable prices), you can purchase a very functional "ready-made" instrument for about $150. A stick from any of today's large manufacturers of cues will be more than sufficient for someone relatively new to the game. Another good option for the new player is to buy a used cue. Most poolrooms either help their customers buy and sell used cues or know where used cues can be purchased. Pool players are notorious for their fickleness and their fanaticism—two qualities that result in lots of barely-used cues becoming available for sale. Advantages of buying a used cue are that they cost less than comparable new cues, and you may have more opportunities to try out a used cue than a new cue before making a decision about whether to buy.

Some players always seem to be buying a new cue. They use their latest cue for awhile, but then quickly sell it (or store it away in the closet) so they can pick up another. As with fans of golf clubs and tennis racquets, many pool players are constantly searching for the magic instrument that will unlock the mystery of better play. Others simply want the newest model. These type of players should not be your role models. Avoid making the game any more difficult than it needs to be by forcing yourself to get used to a different "feel" every time you play. Stay with one cue.

Custom Cues

After you've become more proficient at pool, you may want to trade up to a custom cue. A peculiarity of the state of pool today is that a player can now easily spend more on a cue than on a pool table. All of the custom cue makers produce elaborate examples of what is now recognized as an art. These collectible cues are decorative wonders, often made only for cue-making shows and display. In fact, some of the most expensive examples of these collectible cues are non-functional due to the weight of the exotic woods and inlays chosen for "show" purposes. These cues become simply too heavy for most players to use for playing!

The good news is that there seem to be more cue makers of all types than ever before. These producers run the gamut from one-man shops (craftsmen who fashion virtually every component of a cue by hand) to large manufacturers. An established one-man out-fit with a solid reputation will usually sell cues starting at about $1,000 for a two-piece cue with an extra shaft, while the larger man-ufacturers' prices are more affordable.

If you are looking at new cues, what do you get for the addi-tional expense of a custom cue? Many players (and even non-play-ing collectors) enjoy buying custom cues so that they can have an instrument made of exotic woods and inlays. Although these mate-rials may enhance the beauty of the cue, they do not play any better than maple, the most common cue material. Depending on the type of exotic wood selected, maple may well play better! For those players who prefer heavily inlaid cues, a custom cue can be made to order, with inlays that add to the look and monetary value of a cue, but do not benefit the final product in terms of performance—how the cue plays.

The benefits that you *can* achieve by buying a new custom cue are complete and unlimited choice as to the specifications—weight, balance point, wrap, diameter of the tip (which is usually some-where between twelve and thirteen millimeters), diameter of the cue at the wrap, length (usually 58″ for new cues, although the stan-dard used to be 57″), materials, colors, and more. These types of measurements and choice can enhance your ability to play with the cue since you can select specifications that feel just right for you given your preferences and build. As a pool player accumulates more and more experience on the table, it is common for that player to become more and more discriminating and precise in terms of exactly what type of cue stick he or she has in mind as an ideal. The custom cue maker can deliver that highly personal prod-uct, often times building cues based on designs created by the cus-tomer. Larger manufacturers will generally offer cues in only one length (58″) and one butt diameter size, and the weights offered will often be limited to half-ounce increments (i.e., 19 oz., 19½ oz., 20 oz., 20½ oz., etc.). A custom maker, however, can make your cue 56″ long, extra slim or thick in diameter at the wrap, 18⅞ ounces in weight, and with a tip diameter of 12⅜ mm., if that's how you want it.

A custom cue maker will spend whatever time is necessary to hand-pick the raw materials, design the cues thoughtfully, cut the component pieces to the finest tolerances possible, and then fit those components together so carefully that each inlay and each place where pieces are fitted together is perfectly straight, proportional, and razor-edge sharp. All of this takes time, obviously, and the custom maker cannot possibly match the output of the large manufacturers. For this reason, the custom cues will always carry a higher price tag, but that may be worthwhile for accomplished players willing to pay a premium for that level of quality.

• Chalk •

Most people don't think much about chalk—until they miscue because they forgot to chalk their cue. It is virtually impossible to chalk your cue too frequently. Some players chalk before each and every shot. You should chalk on at least every other shot. Besides making sure that the tip gets a good grip on the cue ball, chalking your cue is a good way to force yourself to pause momentarily to think things over before taking your next shot.

When you're playing well, you may not even notice how often you are chalking your cue. That is because chalking, when you are on your game, becomes as much a part of your rhythm as taking practice strokes and stroking the cue ball.

The correct way to apply chalk is to gently brush it across the entire width of the tip. Not all good players do so, but it is wise to look over the tip after chalking, to make sure you have covered the entire surface. Do not grind the chalk onto your tip, however. Applying too much chalk won't improve your play, will eventually make the table filthy as the excess chalk flakes off as you hit the cue ball, and will cause more chalk to cling to the surface of the balls. When residual chalk comes between the cue ball and an object ball, or a ball and the table surface, the balls don't react the normal way (sometimes described as "skidding"), causing missed shots.

• Keep it Clean •

Caring for a cue and a table is a matter of common sense and courtesy. Even if you are playing in a poolroom, rather than on your own table, you should maintain habits that keep the arena in top condition for your opponent, yourself, and the next player.

When placing the chalk on the rail of the table, avoid putting it face down, which will leave bits of chalk on the rail that are bound to end up on everyone's hands and clothes. If your hands get sticky and you like to apply powder to your hands when you play, make sure you apply it far away from the table, and dust off the excess before your next shot. Also, make sure no powder is left on your hands when you rack the balls.

Room owners hate when players or spectators sit on pool tables . . . and for good reason. Sitting on tables puts pressure on the cushions, which are adjusted to a very precise height so that the balls bank off the cushions properly. Sitting on the rails can incur an expensive repair.

• Must You Accessorize? •

Buying a pool cue is optional. If you do buy a cue, however, the one accessory you must purchase is a cue case. Once in a while, you will see someone who has spent time and money to pick up a cue, but carries the cue in the plastic sheath it came in. This is lunacy since you can buy a good soft cue case for about thirty-five dollars. Starting at about fifty dollars, you can purchase a hard case, which is recommended as better protection for any cue that means anything to you.

An innovation not available in the days when Paul Newman and Jackie Gleason were shooting it out in *The Hustler* is that most cue cases today come with shoulder straps as either optional or standard equipment. Since the point of a case is to protect your cue, anything that makes it less likely that you will accidentally drop the case, such as a shoulder strap, is a good idea. These days, cue cases also usually come with storage pouches for stowing chalk and other accessories.

When it comes to playing pool, no accessory other than a case for your cue is vital. The past greats of the game—Willie Hoppe,

Ralph Greenleaf, and all the others—never needed seventeen types of shaft-polishing products, tip groomers, bridge heads, or gloves to play, and they somehow managed.

On the other hand, if you have a particular personal characteristic, such as sweaty hands, or a particular concern, such as the need to keep the shaft of your cue perfectly clean at all times, a glove for playing pool may make perfect sense. Some of the tools available to keep the tip of the cue rough (so that chalk adheres to it) are also handy, since these gadgets are usually designed to be more portable than a file, the tool of choice decades ago. An ordinary file or a piece of coarse sandpaper, however, folded over several times so that it is fairly stiff, works just fine as a tip scuffer. Do not scuff the tip by *scraping* it with the file or sandpaper. Instead, *roll* the file or sandpaper against the tip, starting at the edge of the tip and working your way towards the center. As you get closer to the center of the tip, you will not need to roll the file or sandpaper as much in order to rough up the surface.

One way to think about whether you need a particular pool accessory is to think in terms of whether having the accessory will help you to worry less or cause you to worry more. For example, if you are very particular about your chalk and you constantly worry about whether the chalk cube you are using will be to your liking, then perhaps one of those chalk-toting gadgets is just the thing for you, to help you focus on playing the game. On the other hand, if you are used to picking up whatever piece of chalk is lying on the rail closest to you, and owning a chalk carrier will become nothing more than a distraction, then getting a chalk carrier makes no sense for you . . . even if it is the latest rage in your poolroom.

• Caring for Your Cue •

While coarse sandpaper works fine on the tip of a cue, *never* use ordinary sandpaper on any other part of a cue. Some players use extremely fine grades of sandpaper—grade 600 or finer (the higher the number, the finer the grade)—to clean and smooth out the shaft of their cues. Even this common practice should be kept to a minimum. The better method for keeping the shaft of a cue clean and smooth is to avoid letting excessive dirt and grime build up in the first place, by wiping the shaft of the cue after each time you play with a damp cloth or paper towel, followed by a dry cloth or paper towel. Don't wait until the dirt and chalk build up to the point where you must resort to strong chemical cleansers or a professional cleaning.

In terms of caring for the tip of the cue, the most important step is to rough it periodically in the manner discussed above. Also check to see if the outside edge of the tip is starting to spread. If the tip has spread only slightly beyond the edge of the ferrule, you can burnish the outside edge of the tip by rubbing it with a piece of leather or a plain piece of paper. Provided you take care to avoid scratching the ferrule, you can also get the tip flush with the ferrule by using sandpaper—again, grade 600 or finer. If the tip has spread well beyond the ferrule, you must first trim off the excess with a sharp knife. Then smooth the outside edge with some 600 sandpaper, and finally, burnish the edge of the tip.

As for the butt section of the cue, because this portion of the cue (other than the wrap) is generally covered by some type of wood finish, all you need to do is wipe it occasionally with ordinary furniture wax. Any of the common spray waxes is acceptable. Don't use anything that contains any type of solvent. If the butt of your cue has a linen or nylon wrap, as most do, you need only wipe the wrap with a damp cloth occasionally to keep it clean. Make sure the cloth is not too wet since you do not want the wrap or the wood beneath it to absorb excess moisture. After that, wipe the wrap again with a clean, dry cloth. Make sure you wipe it in a spiraling motion, following the same direction as the cords of the wrap.

If you are playing with your own personal cue, be careful when using the mechanical bridge (the implement that allows you to extend your cue for shots that you cannot reach with just your hands) found in the poolrooms. If it is metal or if it is badly scratched (or both), a bridge can put a long, possibly irreparable, gouge in the shaft of your cue. Before trying a mechanical bridge that you have not used before, take your finger and run it across the groove where the cue will be resting. Check for ragged edges on the bridge. If you find any, use a different bridge or play the shot using a house cue.

To avoid any unfortunate accidents with the mechanical bridge, some players carry their own bridge heads (the part of the bridge on which the cue actually rests), which slip onto the tip of a house cue. Special bridge heads are generally far superior to the common bridge heads found in your local poolroom in terms of stability, and in terms of the options the bridge heads provide for where the cue can be placed. Of course, you will also be assured that the bridge head you bring with you to the poolroom will not mar the shaft of your cue. If you use the bridge often, buying a bridge head may be a good idea so that you can achieve these benefits.

Sometimes, no matter how careful you try to be with your cue, you will bump it against something and make a dent. If the dent is in the butt of the cue, do not try to repair it yourself. Either live with it or send it back to the manufacturer to be refinished. (Spending the money to refinish a cue is probably worthwhile only after you have accumulated a number of dents or scratches.)

A dent in the shaft of your cue is fairly simple to fix. Just apply a tiny piece of wet tissue or paper towel to the affected area, then put it aside to wait for the wood on the shaft to absorb the water and swell. Then take a piece of paper or thin cardboard and rub it back and forth across the spot on the shaft that has raised up due to the water, and burnish the shaft of the cue back to its original proportions. A gouge or a scratch in the shaft, as opposed to a dent, is a more serious problem. If your shaft becomes scratched, take it to whoever made the cue, or to a qualified cue repair service, to find out what, if anything, can be done to repair the shaft.

• The Essentials •

1. Pay attention to the particular qualities of the pool table on which you are playing. Keep these qualities in mind during the course of your game or practice session so you will be able to make necessary adjustments.
2. When selecting a cue, make sure the tip is properly shaped.
3. If you plan to play pool regularly, buy your own cue stick so that you can use the same cue every time you play.

3

That Critical 20 Percent— The Mechanics of Playing Pool

I t's said that 80 percent of pocket billiards is mental. While that may be so, in a game as demanding as this one can be, perfecting the 20 percent of the game that is physical and mechanical is very important.

If a player is burdened with a fundamental mechanical flaw, the mental aspect of the game never comes fully into play. You may possess the greatest pool mind that ever existed, but you will never become a good player. For that reason, it is critical that you become fully capable and confident in the manner in which you deliver the tip of your cue through each shot (known as the "stroke"), and in every other physical part of the game that leads up to a good stroke.

The fundamental mechanics of a pool stroke can be categorized in terms of how you will need to stand (stance and torso position), how to set one hand on the table (known as the "bridge hand") and the other on the cue (the "rear" hand), and how to strike the ball (the mechanics of the stroke itself).

• Stance and Torso Position •

The next time you are in your local poolroom, take a look at how others stand while delivering a stroke. You will notice that, even among the better players, there exists great variety in terms of how different players stand at the table.

Some players are bent very low over the cue, while others are practically standing straight up, barely bending over the cue at all. Some players stand quite a bit sideways relative to the cue ball (these players adopt what, in baseball, would be called a "closed" stance—with their front foot almost directly in front of their rear foot). Other players position their bodies so that their torsos are practically facing the cue ball with their front foot barely ahead of the rear foot, adopting an "open" stance. How close or how far apart a player keeps his or her legs also varies greatly. Many players (especially the taller ones) tend to keep their feet quite far apart, while other players keep their legs closer together.

If nothing else, this should reassure you that when you get down into your own stance, no one is going to come running over to your table to point out that you are doing something wrong. At the same time, how you stand at the table is important. How *should* you stand at the table?

There are important elements that all good players share when it comes to their stance and torso position. At the root of all good pool stances are the qualities that allow for accuracy (which includes consistency), and unrestricted delivery of a proper stroke.

Allowing for accuracy and consistency boils down to stability in the shooting stance. A good player is solid at the table. Keeping this quality in mind is instructive in terms of how far apart you should keep your legs in the stance. If your legs are too close together, the base your legs provide will not be sufficiently solid. For this reason, the legs should generally be about shoulder-width apart. Depending on your particular body, you may be more comfortable with your legs even a little further apart. For taller players, a somewhat wider stance allows the head to get a little lower over the cue.

The positioning of the feet should allow your rear hand to travel in a straight line through the stroke (illustration 4). This means that, for most players, the torso should not be completely sideways to the cue nor perpendicular to it. Stance is largely a

Illustration 4

matter of comfort. Some great players adopt shooting stances that are awkward for most people. One of the most famous players of all time, Willie Hoppe, was an excellent example of this. He played using a side-arm delivery that worked wonderfully for him. Countless players imitated him, and made themselves miserable until they settled into a more conventional style better suited to their individual body types. For beginning players, I recommend adopting a stance like the one in illustration 4.

By contrast, in illustration 5, the player is almost completely sideways to her cue. For most players, this is uncomfortable and won't allow for a straight follow-through. In illustration 6, the player is nearly perpendicular to her cue. Some of the top professionals (generally pros with a background in the game of snooker) adopt this stance. Even so, this posture is uncomfortable for most players. The exact position your body should adopt to allow your rear hand motion to follow through in a straight line may not be exactly like illustration 4. It will probably be much closer to the stance shown in illustration 4, however, than those shown in illustrations 5

Illustration 5

or 6. The exact position that suits your body will become more evident to you after you have played enough pool to develop a sense of whether your rear hand is stroking freely and comfortably, straight through the stroke.

The stance should be solid, but all of the solidity should come from the legs and how the torso is balanced over the legs. The pool stance is definitely *not* a three-point stance. None of the weight of the body should be resting on the bridge hand. Instead, the body should be in balance from the legs alone, with the bridge hand supporting only the weight of that hand and the cue. Whatever you do, don't lean on the bridge hand. Allow your legs to completely support your body. The bridge hand's job is solely to stabilize and aim the cue stick into the proper spot on the cue ball.

Your stance should be solid enough to allow you to withstand a light shove from any direction without any loss in balance. If you get down into your stance and do not feel that complete sense of balance, adjust your stance and try again. Never settle for an unsatisfactory stance. The stance is the foundation of your stroke, and, like a building, the stroke is bound to falter if the foundation is

Illustration 6

shaky. It is not impossible to deliver a good stroke while your body is leaning to one side or another, but a poor stance will make your odds of success with the stroke much less than what they should be.

Some players keep their heads very low over their cue sticks, which they argue is an advantage in aiming. Many other players have excelled with a nearly erect stance. In general, you should try to keep your head as low to the cue as you can comfortably accomplish. Do not try to adopt an extremely low stance if you do not feel right doing so. Note that even though it is generally advisable to assume as low a stance as possible, for some shots it will be necessary for you to adopt a more erect stance. When the cue ball and the object ball at which you are shooting are close together, for example, you will not be able to see the shot properly if you are too low in your stance. In those types of situations, as well as others (such as bridging over an object ball), you will need to stand fairly straight up simply to see where the correct contact point is on the object ball.

The quality of a stance which allows for accuracy and unrestricted delivery of an effective stroke is proper alignment. All good players realize that the first part of aiming any stroke is to "aim" with the feet and stance. This means finding your normal stance relative to the shot you are about to shoot *before* you lower your head and start taking practice strokes.

Before your bridge hand touches the cloth, you should be sighting the shot and aligning your body and feet so that you can place your bridge hand down at the precise spot that allows you to release a stroke through the exact line you deem necessary to make the shot. Never stay down in your stance and adjust your aim by using only your arms and hands! If the stance does not feel right and an adjustment must be made, make the adjustment right away—before you start your practice strokes (or as soon into your practice strokes as you notice that your body is not perfectly aligned). In this way, you will know that every time you actually stroke the cue ball you will be in perfect balance and alignment.

It's essential that your stance positions your head exactly over your cue, whether you keep your head low or high. While I advocate that you keep your chin directly over the cue, some players align their heads so that one of their eyes—the "dominant eye" that they principally use for aiming—is over the cue. The important fundamental is that you keep your head precisely above your cue in the same manner on each and every shot. Two examples are provided in illustrations 7 and 8.

When a player is in a slump, the problem can often be traced to head position. Without realizing it, the slumping player has altered his or her head position and is missing shots simply because he or she no longer sees the shots properly. Check your head position in a mirror from time to time. Memorize what it looks like and what it feels like when your head is lined up directly over your cue. (You don't need a pool table to practice your stance—a dinner table or a desktop will do!) Then, when you're actually playing, you will find it easier to get into a position where your eyes are perfectly situated to aim your shots.

• Hand Position •

When a pool hustler is scanning the room to figure out whom he can beat and by how much, one of the first things he looks for is a player's hand position. (For that matter, when a pool hustler is trying to look like a weak player he will often act the part by using awkward hand positions.) What this tells us is that the way a player positions his or her bridge hand and rear hand says a great deal about whether he or she possesses the proper mechanics.

How you place your hands when preparing to shoot is one of the most important physical elements of playing pool. What you do with your bridge hand and your rear hand directly affects both your accuracy and your stroke. Since the physical part of pool pretty much comes down to these two elements, the importance of the correct positioning of your bridge hand and rear hand cannot be overemphasized.

There is no rule for which hand should be used as your bridge hand. Overwhelmingly, however, right-handed players bridge the cue with their left hand, and left-handed players use their right hand to bridge the cue. (It is a very good idea to become adept at shooting with either hand so that you can shoot comfortably from anywhere on the table. Whether you are an advanced player or a beginner, developing this skill will be a great advantage.)

Illustration 7

Illustration 8

• The Rear Hand •

The rear hand is the hand that actually delivers the stroke through the cue ball. In pool, the rear hand plays the same part that the dominant hand (i.e., the right hand for right-handed players) plays in baseball, golf, and tennis. In the truest sense, the rear hand in pool controls the stroke.

Many beginners hold the cue too far back or too far forward with the rear hand. Either error can interfere with one of the keys to good form—a level stroke. Holding the cue too far back causes it to move up and down a lot during the delivery of the stroke. Another problem with holding the cue stick too far back with the rear hand is that it makes developing touch on all types of shots much more difficult. Since the rear hand is already in an awkward position and the shoulders are contorted by holding the cue too far back, developing the touch needed to play pool well is nearly impossible. (Note: Figuring out whether your rear hand placement is correct involves more than merely looking at whether your hand is on the wrap of the cue, behind the wrap, or before it, since so much depends on the build of the player. For a tall player using a standard 58-inch cue, the rear hand will probably be towards the back of the wrap, and perhaps behind the wrap. The test for proper rear hand placement is discussed below.)

Holding the cue too far *forward* with the rear hand is a much less common mistake, but a mistake nonetheless. When the cue is held in this way, the stroke is inhibited since following through becomes awkward. (In a sense, when you are holding the cue too far forward, you are starting from a position that is part-way through a correct follow-through. Holding the cue too far forward thus leaves you unable to finish off your stroke completely.)

There is a simple way to check that you are holding the cue at the proper point—neither too far back on the cue stick nor too far forward. Address the cue ball as if you are about to take a shot, placing the tip of your cue as close to the cue ball as possible without touching it. When you're in this position, the rear hand should be hanging *directly below your elbow*. With your rear hand in this position, you are in a position to take a full backswing and a complete follow-through. Also, your shoulders are neither stretched too far apart (which happens when the cue is gripped too far back) nor pinched together (which happens when the cue is gripped too far forward).

Notice that we have talked about how the rear hand should be "hanging" directly below the elbow. This means that the rear hand should be holding the butt of the cue with a light touch. The rear hand does not "grip" the cue or "grasp" it. In fact, the entire rear hand does not even hold the butt of the cue since the ring finger and pinkie of the rear hand do not support any of the weight of the cue stick. Instead, the cue stick is supported by the other three fingers (although the ring finger and the pinkie may be touching the butt end of the cue). Most of the weight of the cue is supported by the thumb and index finger.

Again, the goal for the mechanics of your game is to allow you to develop a fine sense of touch. Gripping the cue firmly with the rear hand makes developing touch impossible. Gripping the cue tightly in this manner also tends to create an up-and-down sawing motion when the cue is stroked back and forth. This problem is similar to holding the cue stick too far back. Both of these mechanical flaws render it impossible for a player to create a level, fluid stroke. Even though it's popular with the hustlers, unless you want to remain a mediocre player for life, hold the rear of the cue gently, and avoid keeping the rear hand too far back on the butt of the cue stick.

• The Bridge Hand •

A bridge is the formation of the hand that you use to support the shaft of the cue. How a player forms a bridge is another telltale sign of whether he or she has good mechanics. While the rear hand controls the stroke, the bridge hand controls how accurately that stroke is applied. If you have the best stroke in the world but you cannot get the tip of your cue to contact the cue ball at the proper point, you will never enjoy any success at this game. The bridge hand delivers the stroke to the proper point on the cue ball. The bridge hand is about precision.

The first element to forming a bridge hand that allows you to apply your stroke precisely is making sure that the bridge is solid. The bridge hand must be stable and steady. This is one of the reasons why stance and torso position is so important. If your entire body is unbalanced you cannot make a steady bridge. Consequently, your shots will lack accuracy. Just like your body position, your bridge hand should be a model of stability. This should be the case no matter what type of bridge you are making, and there are a number of different types.

You will need to become comfortable with at least four basic types of bridges: (1) a bridge for when the cue ball is resting in the open field of the table, away from the rails; (2) a bridge for when the cue ball is about four to six inches off of a rail; (3) a bridge for when the cue ball is "frozen" against the rail (that is, the cue ball is directly against the rail) and you want to shoot away from the rail, not along it; and (4) a bridge for when you need to shoot over a ball. Most players use more than these four basic types of bridges, but in most cases, the other types of bridges are merely adaptations or variations of these basic bridge types. Except perhaps for the rail bridge, you will want to fan out the fingers on your bridge hand to provide a broad, stable base no matter which type of bridge you are making.

The bridge you will use most often is the bridge for situations when the cue ball is not near a rail. In those situations, you will be able to put your bridge hand behind the cue ball comfortably. Most, but not all, players prefer a "closed" bridge for these situations. For a closed bridge, the index finger of the bridge hand loops over the cue stick, with the cue stick sliding over the middle finger of the bridge hand (illustration 9).

The advantage of this closed bridge is that it is very stable. The cue stick will not move much from its intended target. Just about every good player uses the closed bridge at times, and some use it almost exclusively. A difficulty with the closed bridge, however, is that it is not always easy for new players to form. A fairly simple method for learning to form a closed bridge is to make an "okay" sign with the bridge hand—connecting the tip of your index finger to the tip of your thumb, and then pulling back your index finger and thumb until the point at which they meet touches your middle finger at roughly midway along its length. Examples are shown in illustrations 10 and 11. After you have gotten used to forming the closed bridge in this manner, try forming it around the cue stick.

The closed bridge should be formed as snugly around the cue stick as possible while still allowing the cue to pass smoothly through your fingers. If the bridge is too loose, the cue stick may stray from the intended target on the cue ball. If the bridge is too tight, it will interfere with your delivery of the stroke.

You should also become comfortable with an open bridge. In the open bridge, the index finger does not loop over the cue stick. Instead, the shaft of the cue stick simply glides along a notch formed between the index finger and the thumb (illustration 12). Although the open bridge is not quite as stable as the closed bridge, many players favor it over the closed bridge simply because they never learned to make the closed bridge properly or comfortably. Some players also find that the loop formed by the index finger with a closed bridge gets in the way of trying to sight the cue stick.

Practice using both of these styles of bridge so that you will have the flexibility to take advantage of the benefits of each. For example, the open bridge is often more natural to use than the closed bridge when you must stretch to reach for a shot that is a good distance across the table. The closed bridge, however, will give you

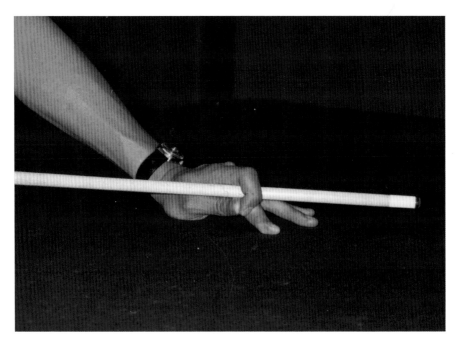

Illustration 9

greater stability and security, and is especially helpful when you must apply any type of extreme spin to the cue ball.

When the cue ball is four to six inches away from a rail and you're shooting away from the rail, you will need to use a different type of bridge. Illustrations 13 and 14 depict how to form a very solid and simple bridge for these types of situations. You form this bridge by first laying your thumb on the rail and allowing the cue stick to rest on the rail against the edge of your thumb (illustration 13); then, by placing your middle and index fingers on either side of the shaft of the cue stick (illustration 14).

The third type of bridge you'll need is for situations when the cue ball is frozen, or nearly frozen, against a rail and you're shooting away from the rail. See illustrations 15 and 16 for two examples. Bridging the cue in these situations poses problems because the entire cue ball is not available; you're limited to stroking just the uppermost part of the ball. The most important goals to keep in mind for this type of bridge are to keep the bridge as low as possible and to keep the cue stick as level as possible. Notice that this bridge is

Illustration 10

merely an adaptation of the open bridge shown in illustration 12. Here, the key is to keep the cue stick as level as possible.

When using the bridge shown in illustration 17, make sure that the rear hand stays down! A common mistake at all levels of play is to raise the rear hand and to strike down on the cue ball. "Jacking up" the cue stick in this manner greatly reduces your accuracy by adding accidental side-spin to the stroke. Keep the cue and the stroke level, and you will develop consistency even when faced with the need to form a rail bridge.

The last of the four basic bridges is used when you are trying to bridge over an obstructing ball. This is perhaps one of the most difficult situations in pool. The bridge used for bridging over a ball is always an open bridge. Almost everyone makes this type of bridge a little differently, but the common element is that the hand is supported principally by the index finger and pinkie, as shown in illustration 18. The middle and ring fingers are then bent so that those fingers can also provide some support for the bridge. The thumb is curved upward and provides a groove for the cue to rest upon. As

Illustration 11

with every other type of bridge, when bridging over balls, strive to keep your bridge hand as stable and solid as possible. It is usually helpful to keep the wrist up away from the bed of the table. Again, the stance must be completely stable as well. Here, you will be forced to stroke downward onto the cue ball. That is part of what makes shooting from this position so difficult. You should still strive to keep the cue and the stroke as level as possible, however, when bridging over a ball.

Some shots can only be reached with the mechanical bridge. Even the pros disagree on how often a player should use this tool. I recommend learning to shoot with either hand so that you'll rarely need the mechanical bridge. Others argue that you're better off getting used to the mechanical bridge rather than trying to play with the opposite hand. Either way, there will be times when you *must* use the bridge.

As with any shot, start by approaching the shot so that your head is aligned over the intended path of the cue ball. Then place

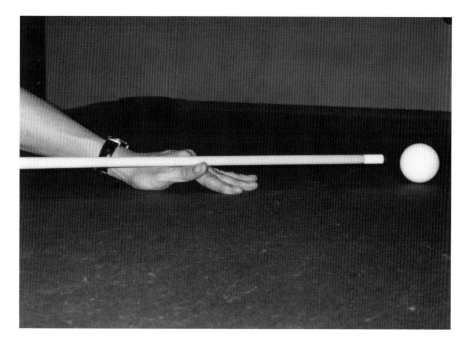

Illustration 12

the bridge head. Do not hold the handle of the bridge in the air; instead, lay it down and place your hand over it for stability, as shown in illustration 19. Grip the handle of your cue so that the palm of your hand is facing away from you, and, like every other shot, keep your head directly in line with your cue.

Which notch in the bridge head you choose to use will depend upon how high or low you will need to stroke the cue ball. In illustration 20, a low hit on the cue ball is desired. When bridging over object balls, however, you will need to run the cue stick over the highest notch of the bridge head in order to obtain the necessary clearance. Even on the types of shots shown in illustration 21, keep your cue as level as you can. This means that your cue stick should barely clear the obstructing object balls.

The motion for a stroke using the bridge is obviously quite different from your usual stroke. Despite these differences, continue to strive for a relaxed delivery, aimed precisely.

Illustration 13

Illustration 14

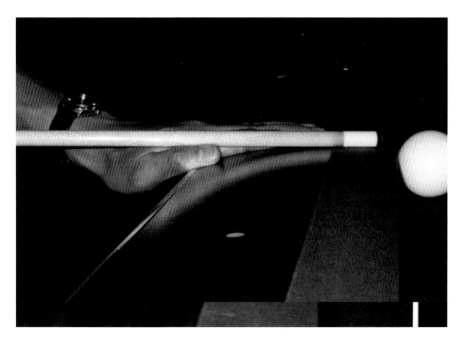

Illustration 15

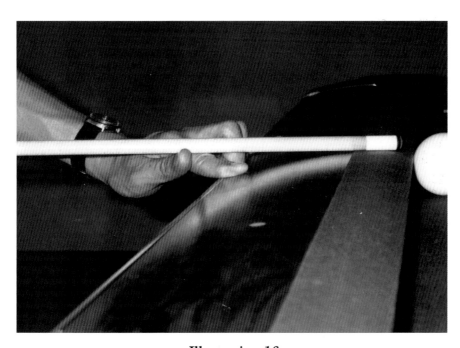

Illustration 16

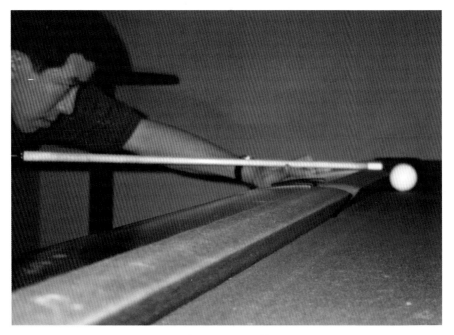

Illustration 17

• The Stroke—What Will Separate You for Life from Every Other Pool Player (Whether You Like It or Not) •

The stroke in billiards should be a simple motion. It is merely the rear hand moving the cue stick forward, aimed at a point focused by the bridge hand. That's all. Yet, a sense of mystique surrounds how the stroke is executed and what the stroke accomplishes. Like the stance, there is unlimited variety in how different players deliver a stroke through the cue ball. The characters hanging around poolrooms everywhere define players by their strokes. Stop by a poolroom for thirty seconds and you'll hear different players' strokes described, in flattering or unflattering terms: This player has a "precise" stroke; that player suffers from a "hitch" (an out-of-place hesitation or movement) in his stroke; another has an "even, soft stroke," while another has a "powerful" stroke; an accom-

Illustration 18

Illustration 19

plished player gets nice "action" (deliberate spin) from her stroke; and so on.

What qualities should be embodied in the stroke? Smoothness and consistency. Let's address each of these qualities separately.

Illustration 20

Keeping the rear arm, hand, and wrist relaxed and loose are keys to a smooth stroke. In tense moments, this is not always easy. Nerves and adrenaline can sometimes make a player with a normally sound stroke deliver an awful example of a stroke—stiff, awkward, and uneven. A good way to check whether your body is relaxed enough to deliver a smooth stroke is to silently ask yourself if you can feel the weight of the cue stick pulling downward on the fingers of your rear hand, wrist, and arm. If the answer is "yes," then take your practice strokes (in which the cue tip approaches but does not touch the ball), and let fly. If the answer is "no," jiggle your rear hand until it loosens up and becomes sensitive to the weight of the cue stick. Make sure you feel the heft of the cue stick; then proceed with your practice strokes and the shot itself.

You can also achieve smoothness in your stroke through developing the sense that the weight of the cue stick—not your arm—is supplying the power for the stroke. Imagine that the rules of pool required you to let go of the cue stick with your rear hand just before the end of the stroke. If that were so, the weight of the cue stick

Illustration 21

alone (propelled through your bridge hand) would provide all the power needed to get the cue ball moving. That is the feeling of a relaxed, smooth stroke. Some players develop a sense that the tip of the cue is accelerating through the cue ball during the stroke. Keeping these types of images in mind is surprisingly effective. Whatever you do, never push the cue stick forward or think of the stroke as a pushing type of motion. One of the problems associated with pushing on your stroke is that it is nearly impossible to push the cue through your bridge hand exactly the same way twice. In extreme cases, pushing the cue stick may cause the tip of the cue to maintain contact with the cue ball "more than the momentary time commensurate with a stroked shot," which constitutes a foul. (Billiard Congress of America General Rule 3.24.) An exaggerated push may even cause a "double hit," which is also a foul. (BCA General Rule 3.23.)

The second essential quality of a good stroke is consistency. In sports requiring highly refined touch (billiards and golf immediately come to mind as examples), players seem to complain about one problem above all others—lack of consistency. In purely mental pursuits, such as chess, a lack of consistency can be traced purely to mental problems, such as concentration lapses. Not so in pool. Pool requires you to do something with your body. You must coordinate your mind *and* your body for the goal of putting a white sphere in motion in a very particular fashion in terms of direction, speed, and spin.

Small deviations in the mechanical way you stroke the cue ball can create havoc with how the cue ball behaves on the table. The solution is easy: Keep your mechanics simple. When your pool stroke is economical and consists of very few moving parts, then very little can go wrong. When your pool stroke is made up of many different motions (some balancing out others to varying degrees), any small change can spell disaster. Keep your mechanics simple. Do not get used to incorporating dips or exaggerated hand, wrist, or arm motions into your stroke. Your stroke must be free of this type of extra baggage.

At least in this respect, avoid imitating what you see many players in your local poolroom doing. Players with stylish extras to their strokes are often accomplished, and in other aspects of their games may be fine role models. Keep in mind, however, that these types of players must be constantly playing to maintain their games. All of the little extras to their stroke production invariably haunt them if they take even so much as a day or two off from playing. With a longer layoff, players like these may take months to get back to the point where they can consistently pocket balls and control the cue ball.

For consistency, less is more. The stroke should be a simple, unhurried motion where the cue stick is brought straight backwards and then straight forward. That is all. Nothing more.

Consistency in the stroke (and in pocketing balls) also means consistency in what you do before and during your stroke, and stick to it. An example of a good routine would include the following steps:

1. While standing straight up, determine the precise point at which you will be aiming, and how you want to stroke the cue ball in terms of speed and english (covered in chapter 7).

2. Prepare to get into your stance by "aiming" your feet and body (aligning yourself based on your aiming point).

3. Get into your stance. Is your chin directly above your cue stick? Does your rear hand feel the weight of the cue? Are you 100 percent confident that your body is positioned properly given how you want to stroke the cue ball? If not, go back to step 1. If so, proceed.

4. Take a predetermined number of practice strokes (warm-up strokes in preparation for actually striking the cue ball). Most players take five or six practice strokes, but there is no rule for how many you should take. Don't take so many, however, that you give yourself too much time to dwell on a shot and get nervous. Few players take more than eight practice strokes. Use these strokes as bona fide practice; that is, take them the way you intend to deliver the actual stroke and at the speed you intend to use on the actual stroke. On the last practice stroke, when the tip of your cue is near the cue ball, you should hold it there a moment or two, and ensure that your aim is accurate and your stance is comfortable.[1] Again, if anything feels off—even if you feel

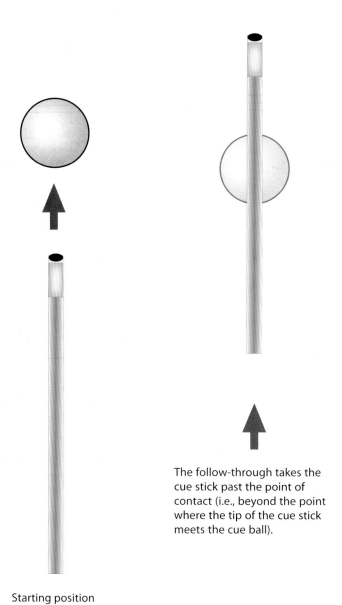

Starting position

The follow-through takes the cue stick past the point of contact (i.e., beyond the point where the tip of the cue stick meets the cue ball).

Illustration 21a

you'll probably make the shot anyway—stand up, and go back to step 1. Every time you take a stroke you want to feel 100 percent confident of your aim and body position.

5.   Stroke the cue ball, ensuring that you accelerate the tip of the cue stick well past the cue ball's original position (the "follow-through"). See illustration 21a.

There is not that much to it. After you've played for a while, your routine will become a part of you and you will not need to over-think each of the steps. Instead, you will be able to focus on the mental aspects of the game. Ideally, your stroke and your routine can become so simple mechanically, and so ingrained, that pool becomes nearly a purely mental exercise for you. The 20 percent of your game that is physical—through its sheer simplicity and purity—will then allow you to achieve new heights in your game, limited only by your imagination and your thinking.

• The Essentials •

1.   Make your stance and your bridge hand as solid and stable as possible.

2.   Keep your rear hand relaxed.

3.   Make sure your stroke remains as simple a motion as possible.

4.   Establish and maintain a routine for how you prepare to stroke the cue ball and how you execute the stroke itself.

---

[1] Some instructors also teach their students to take extra time after taking the cue stick back just before the actual stroke. There is validity in this approach as well, because the cue stick must stop moving after the backswing before it starts moving forward, and many players develop inconsistencies in this transition. I suggest that you do whatever feels rhythmically right for you, which hopefully will translate into a smoother stroke.

4

Aiming Kept Simple—How to Make Your Shots

L et's say that you have perfected the physical side of your game. With your solid stance, solid bridge, and smooth, accurate stroke, you are able to glide the cue ball across the cloth to the exact point you choose. How do we know where the cue ball should be aimed?

This aspect of billiards is the undoing of many players. Although aiming is rather simple, many players make it harder on themselves than is necessary. The solution is plain: *Don't complicate it.*

Remember that making any shot comes down to just three straight lines, as shown in illustration 22: The first line is the cue; the second line connects the cue ball to the proper contact point on the object ball; and the third line connects the object ball to the pocket.

Figuring out where to aim the cue ball is the first step. Once that is done, the other lines fall into place.

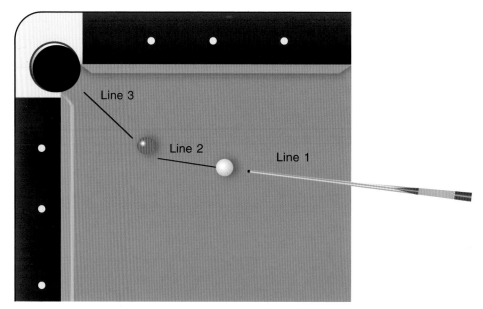

Illustration 22

• The Point of Aim,
the Point of Contact, and the Difference
Between the Two •

Many beginners are confused by the fact that the point at which you aim the cue ball is nearly always different from the point where the cue ball and object ball make contact. The point of aim is where you aim the center of the cue ball. The point of contact is where the two balls actually touch at impact (illustration 23). When you are stroking the cue ball at an object ball, you are dealing with two round objects of a certain diameter, namely, 2¼". For this reason, the *only* time the point of aim and the point of contact are one and the same is when your shot is straight into the pocket (illustration 24).

The difference between the point of aim and the point of contact becomes greater as the shot at which you are aiming becomes less and less straight. Thus, on thin cut shots (extremely angled shots), the point of aim is significantly away from the object ball, as shown in illustration 23.

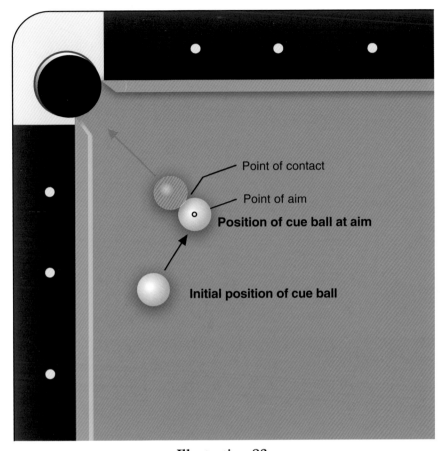

Illustration 23

Once you properly visualize the point of aim, shooting a cut shot is not vastly different from shooting a straight-in shot. In both cases, you must deliver the cue ball to the correct place for the object ball to go in the pocket. If the cue ball makes contact at the proper point, the object ball *must head straight towards the pocket.* (This discussion puts aside, for the time being, the effects of side-spin—often called— "english" and throw—the alteration of the object ball's direction after the cue ball is struck with english.) If, on the other hand, the cue ball makes contact at any other point, you will miss. Once the proper aiming point is selected, all you need to do is make sure you deliver the cue ball to the proper point of aim. In other words, all you must do is make sure line 1 (your cue) and

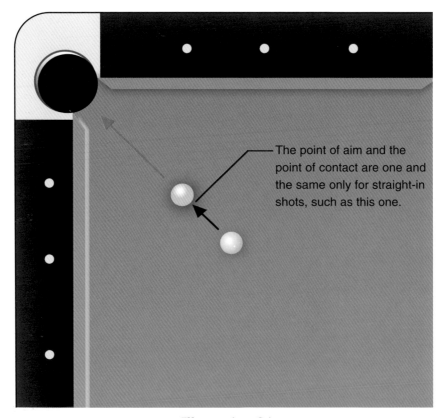

The point of aim and the point of contact are one and the same only for straight-in shots, such as this one.

Illustration 24

line 2 (the desired path of the cue ball) are aligned when you execute the shot.

Remember what we discussed about establishing and sticking to your routine for stroke preparation? Try not to allow the pace of your shot making to be dictated by how "easy" or "difficult" a shot appears to be. Whether you are shooting a short straight-in shot or a near-90 degree cut shot, take whatever time is necessary to visualize the precise point where you must aim the cue ball. Even when faced with a short shot or a relatively straight shot, wait until you have precisely visualized the point of aim before you pull the trigger. If you are having trouble visualizing the shot, stand up and begin again. Even on short- and medium-length straight-in shots, the object ball must be contacted at the proper point.

On these straight shots, just like any other, take the time and effort to precisely choose your point of aim. Don't make the common mistake of taking a shot for granted. Make it a habit to pick out the exact point of aim before you stroke the cue ball—every single time—no matter how easy the shot appears to be.

On the other end of the spectrum, don't overestimate the difficulty of a shot simply because it is an extremely angled (i.e., a thin) cut shot. If you have visualized the precise point of aim, your goal is no different than for any other shot: namely, to deliver the cue ball to the proper point of aim. Take the same number of practice strokes you routinely take, and then execute the shot.

• Finding the Point of Aim Using the Arrow System •

One way to make aiming easier is to use an aiming device to help you pick out the proper point of aim. I came up with a simple device that I call "the Arrow," which helps players to train their eye when aiming the cue ball for a point off of the object ball to pocket cut shots. I have found that the Arrow works particularly well for newer players, who are less accustomed to the difference between the point of aim and the point of contact.

You can make your own Arrow using this book. An actual-size drawing of the Arrow is found in illustration 25. Use this drawing for fashioning your own Arrow out of thin cardboard (such as an index card or business card) or thin plastic. The material you use must not be too thick. (You do not want your Arrow to interfere with the roll of the cue ball on the table.) The dimensions of the Arrow are what make it work. A regulation pocket billiard ball measures 2¼″ in diameter. The full length of the Arrow also measures exactly 2¼″. One-half of the width of a ball is 1⅛″, and the distance from the end of the Arrow to the tip of the interior point is 1⅛″. The distance from the tip of the interior point to the tip of the exterior point is also 1⅛″. These dimensions allow the Arrow to be used as an aiming aid.

For any shot anywhere on the table, place the Arrow so that it is lined up with the intended pocket and so that the interior point is directly under the edge of the object ball, at the precise point where the cue ball must contact the object ball for the shot to be made (illustration 26). The exterior point is now exactly half a

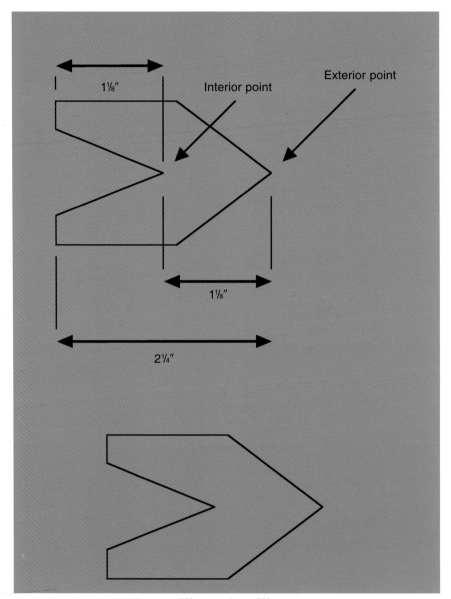

Illustration 25

ball's width away. This exterior point is the aiming point; that is, the point at which you aim the center of the cue ball.

    If you are able to deliver the cue ball so that it rolls over the exterior point of the arrow, the cue ball must contact the object ball at the proper contact point, and the object ball must go in (again,

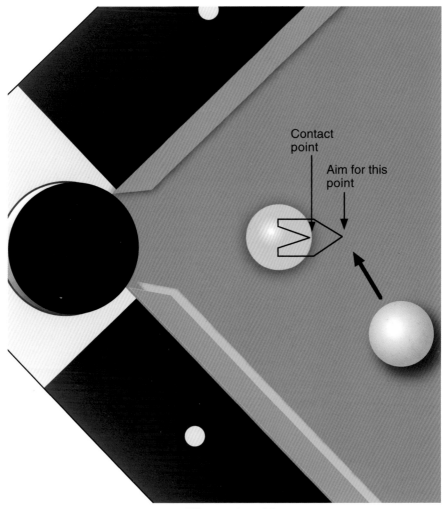

Illustration 26

assuming the absence of english and throw). *This is true no matter where the cue ball is located at the start of the shot.* Being aware of this fact takes some of the mystique out of pocketing balls. Since the point of contact never changes, every shot you see, in a sense, is exactly like the one you just played (illustration 27).

Every player has trouble "seeing," or visualizing, particular shots. One example of a shot that gives many players difficulty is shown in illustration 28. Many players tend to aim this shot too full, and as a result, the shot is undercut and hits the cushion of the foot

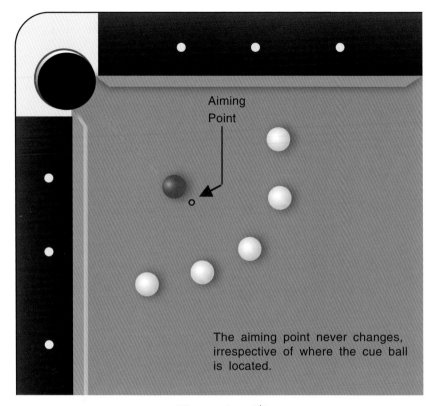

Aiming
Point

The aiming point never changes,
irrespective of where the cue ball
is located.

Illustration 27

rail instead of going into the corner pocket. Practicing these and other troublesome shots five to fifteen times with the Arrow helps to program into your eyes and brain the way to look at such shots. You may miss on your first attempts at a particular shot, but by using the Arrow and examining your results, you will eventually start pocketing the ball. For example, you may notice that you are missing by "undercutting" the shot (i.e., hitting too much of the object ball and thus causing it to roll into the cushion on the near side of the pocket—the foot rail in illustration 28). Or you may notice that you are "overcutting" the shot (i.e., making too thin a hit on the object ball and thus causing it to roll into the cushion on the far side of the pocket—the side rail in illustration 28). By repeating the same shot and examining your results, you will become more comfortable and will be able to locate the aiming and contact points for

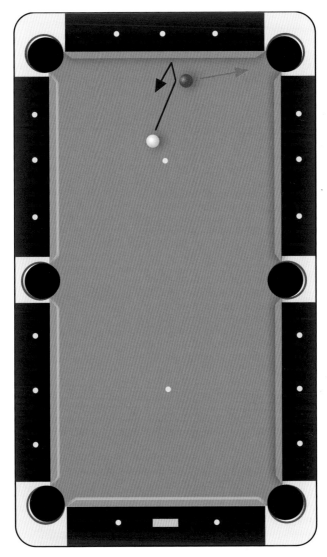

Illustration 28

that particular shot more easily in a game. In other words, you will have taught yourself how to see the shot properly.

In a game situation (when aiming without using the Arrow), always look at each shot from the straight-in perspective. In other words, examine the object ball from the vantage point directly opposite the pocket (illustration 29). Whether you are a beginner or an advanced player, this simple routine reduces misses.

After starting out by using the Arrow for the types of shots described above, you will no doubt find your own applications for this aiming tool. Even after you become very advanced at pool, the Arrow will help to remind you precisely of how you must aim the cue ball to pocket shots.

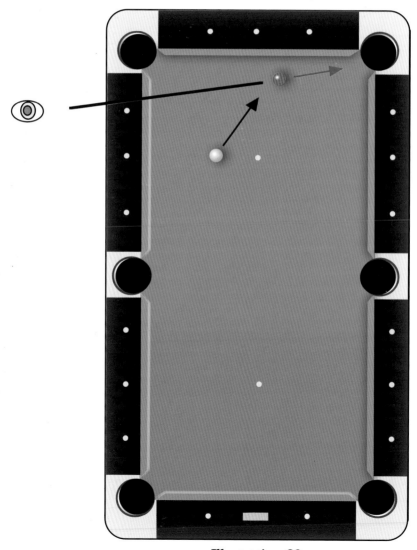

Illustration 29

• Fine-Tuning Your Aiming—When and How to Make Adjustments •

When it comes to pocketing balls, everyone has good days and bad days. Yet the better players seem to improve their pocketing ability during a game even when they've gotten off to a poor start. How do these better players adjust and start making their shots in the heat of competition?

For one thing, all good pool players are observant. When they miss, they're not wasting their time cursing their bad luck. Instead, they're noticing details such as whether they've overcut their shot or undercut it. (Even when they *make* shots, they may notice which side of the pocket the object ball falls into.) The better players also notice whether a particular pocket is "tighter" (narrower) and requires a more precise shot or slower speed, whether a particular part of the table tends to drift one way or the other, and other information that can be applied later in a game. A critical step towards becoming a superb shot maker is becoming aware of and in touch with details like these. Another step is knowing when to make an adjustment and when to leave well enough alone.

If you notice that you are missing the same way time and again (for example, undercutting every missed shot), you must accept that an adjustment is in order. This is sometimes easier said than done. Some players rigidly stick with aiming their shots the same way over and over again because they are convinced that they are aiming their shots correctly. It is important to understand that, each time you play pool, variables—lighting, how much sleep you got the night before, how your nerves and brain happen to be working on a particular day—will cause you to see shots somewhat differently than on other days. When you are having a day where you are undercutting every shot, make a silent commitment to stroke the cue ball only after you have picked out your initial point of aim, and you adjust the point of aim to cut the shot slightly more than where your initial point of aim dictates. Do not aim to overcut the pocket. Instead, aim to cut the shot enough to go into the outside part of the pocket. If you miss, miss by overcutting.

This type of thinking obviously does not eliminate misses, but will improve your shot making as your match progresses. In a way, you should be happy to find out that you are missing shots in a consistent fashion (always overcutting or always undercutting), since you will at least know that an adjustment is in order, and what adjustment is necessary. After making the necessary adjustment, you may find that you do not need to concentrate quite so hard on where to aim and how to adjust, because the aiming becomes more natural—a part of how you're seeing the shots.

Obviously, no adjustment is necessary when you think you know where to aim the cue ball, and you're right! Another time to avoid making an aiming adjustment is when you are missing in an erratic fashion. If you are missing some shots by overcutting and other shots by undercutting, you should first try to figure out whether there is some other type of pattern at play. Maybe you are missing on both sides of the pocket because you are leaving the cue ball in spots where bridging for your shots is more difficult, such as leaving the cue ball against rails, against other balls, or in locations where you have to stretch to play your next shot. If you are able to examine your game to the point where you can pick up on these types of underlying problems, you can then focus on the solution— for example, adjusting your cue ball speed or adjusting how you get from one shot to the next.

If your pocketing problems don't fall into such a neat category, you may be missing in a variety of different ways because of a problem with your mechanics. If that is the case, adjusting how you aim the cue ball only makes the problem worse by throwing into the mix yet another variable. Instead, run through a checklist of mechanical fundamentals: (1) Is your head directly over your cue? (2) Are you making sure that you do not shoot until your body position feels completely solid at the table? (3) Is your bridge firm? (4) Is your rear hand relaxed? (5) Is your rear hand directly under your elbow at the start of the stroke? (6) Are you keeping your head and body in position all the way until the object ball reaches the pocket?

When you are playing great, never second-guess yourself. Just try to maintain the same state of mind, staying focused yet relaxed. If things are not going your way, however, they are unlikely to change unless you modify your approach. Learning when you need to make an adjustment, and becoming observant enough at the table to diagnose what change must be made, will make you a dangerous opponent.

• Combination Shots •

In combination shots, the cue ball does not directly contact the object ball to be pocketed. Instead, the cue ball hits one object ball, and that first object ball (or a second or third, etc.) eventually contacts the ball to be pocketed.

In certain games, such as straight pool, playing combination shots should be avoided at almost any cost. Yet in other games, such as nine-ball, being able to pocket a combination shot is a critical skill. Even in straight pool, there will be times when taking a combination shot is preferable to playing other available shots or playing a safety. For this reason, learning how to aim combination shots is a must.

Good players recognize, however, that combinations are more difficult than they appear. This is because the margin for error is tiny compared to non-combination shots. The pockets on most pool tables are more than twice as wide as the width of a ball. Thus, many non-combination shots are pocketed even though the cue ball does not meet the object ball at the precise spot intended.

Combination shots are another story. In a two-ball combination shot, the cue ball must contact the first object ball very precisely so that the first object ball can then travel to, or very near, the correct contact point in order to pocket the second object ball. Small errors in where the cue ball meets the first object ball translate into missing the pocket with the second object ball by a wide margin. The precision required for combination shots means that the further the distance between the first and second object balls, the more difficult the shot—unless the ball to be pocketed is very close to the intended pocket.

Let's look at the most common type of combinations, two-ball combinations. In illustration 30, the cue ball contacts ball X, which rolls into ball Y, which is then pocketed in the corner pocket. With combination shots, you are in essence using two cue balls: the white ball and the first object ball (ball X in illustration 30). When faced with a combination shot, first examine the shot as if ball X is the cue ball. Look at ball Y from the straight-in perspective, as we did back in illustration 29, just like any other shot. Pick out the precise point on ball Y where contact must be made. Then, as if ball X is your cue ball, determine where you must aim ball X in order to line up for

Illustration 30

the correct point of aim for ball Y. Next, repeat the whole process using the actual cue ball as the cue ball. Look at ball X from directly behind where you would need to contact ball X so that it rolls into the proper point of contact for ball Y. Pick out the precise point on ball X where contact must be made. Then, determine where the cue ball must be aimed in order to line up for the correct point of aim for ball X.

Since being off by just a degree or two on ball X will translate into ball Y falling off course substantially, it is important to avoid shooting too hard on your combination shots. It is common for combination shots to be missed by the object ball rattling off one of the edges of the pockets. If those same shots were executed with a slightly softer hit, some of them would roll into the pocket despite touching the edge of the pocket on the way in.

Another way to pocket balls is to carom the cue ball off of one object ball so that the cue ball rolls into, and pockets, a second object ball. An old-fashioned term for a carom is a "billiard." Pocketing caroms requires an understanding of where the cue ball will travel after contacting an object ball, a subject addressed in chapter 6.

• The Essentials •

1. Keep in mind that the point of aim and the point of contact are different except with straight-in shots.

2. Until you become comfortable with how to aim all types of shots, use the Arrow to reinforce in your memory where the cue ball must be aimed in order to pocket shots that are giving you trouble.

3. Once you have picked out a precise point of aim, do not complicate the aiming process. Instead, focus on making sure that your cue is in line with the line between the cue ball and the point of aim.

4. If you have picked out the precise point of aim, and you have checked to make sure that your cue is aligned with the line between the cue ball and the point of aim, do not dwell unnecessarily on the shot. Take your regular number of practice strokes, and then deliver your stroke through the cue ball.

5. Expect to make your combination shots. Treat the first object ball you contact as the cue ball when lining up your shot. Make sure that you do not stroke your combination shots with excessive speed.

5

Three Keys to Cue Ball Control: The Stop Shot, the Follow Shot, and the Draw Shot

T
he best players nearly always seem to be able to position the cue ball favorably for their next shot ("playing position" or "getting shape," as it is sometimes called). One of the most exciting moments in any pool player's life is when he or she no longer merely pockets balls but also learns how to play position for the next shot. Suddenly, pool is transformed from a random selection of shots to a game where you can control what your next shot, and your next series of shots, will be. After that, the greatest thrills offered by pool are within your reach, including "running out" (pocketing in succession all of the balls needed to win the game so that your opponent never gets another chance to shoot).

Mastery of position play begins with only three key shots: the stop shot, the follow shot, and the draw shot. When the cue ball, the object ball, and the pocket are all aligned, a stop shot enables the

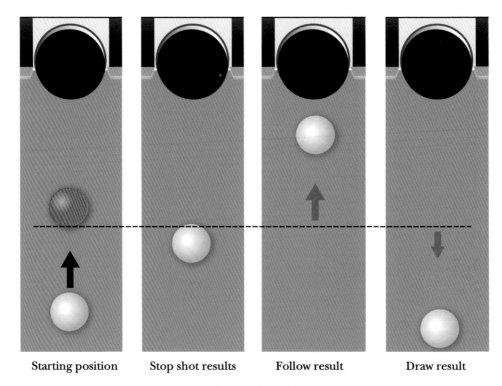

| Starting position | Stop shot results | Follow result | Draw result |

Illustration 31

cue ball to stop dead in its tracks after contacting the object ball (illustration 31). A follow shot is when the player causes the cue ball to roll forward (or "follow") after making contact with the object ball. The draw shot, many players' favorite, causes the cue ball to retreat from the object ball after contact, as depicted in illustration 31.

• Your Reference Point: The Short Stop Shot •

Position play begins and ends with the stop shot. No matter how proficient you become at pool, you will always rely on the short stop shot. Learning to stop the cue ball is not difficult and should be one of the first skills you master. Set up the cue ball and one object ball as shown in illustration 32. With the cue ball this close to the object ball, a stop shot is accomplished with a center-ball hit—that is, make sure the tip of your cue stick contacts the cue ball at the

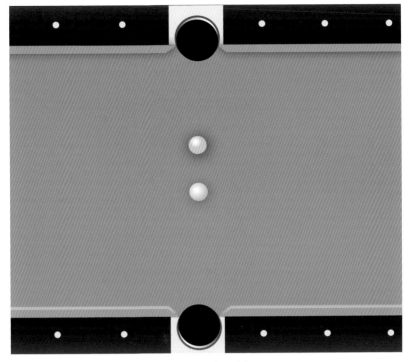

Illustration 32

equator of the cue ball—not high or low (illustration 33). A medium speed is all that is necessary. On this particular shot, stroke the cue ball with enough authority to cause the object ball to hit the back of the pocket (not merely drop off the lip of the pocket), but not slam in.

On *all* shots, the tip of your cue stick should follow through beyond the point where the tip of your cue contacts the cue ball. The stop shot is no exception. If you are having trouble getting the cue ball to stop on a dime, first make sure that you are following through smoothly after contact. If the cue ball still lurches forward, try aiming the tip of your cue stick slightly lower.

Understanding how the stop shot works will help you to execute this critical shot consistently. A cue ball will stop—indeed, it *must* stop—when the shot is straight-in as in illustration 32 (this allows all of the energy of the cue ball to be transferred to the object ball); and at impact, the cue ball is free of any forward or reverse rotation. When the distance between the cue ball and object ball is

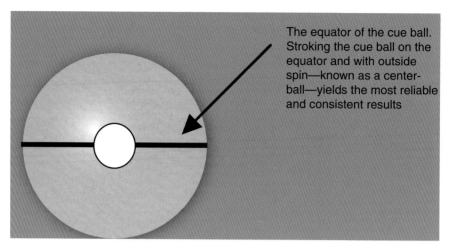

The equator of the cue ball. Stroking the cue ball on the equator and with outside spin—known as a center-ball—yields the most reliable and consistent results

Illustration 33

short, a foot or less, and a proper stop shot is executed, the cue ball will be free of any rotation at impact because it never had any. The cue ball merely *slides* across the cloth over its short path to the object ball.

You can observe this sliding phenomenon by using a striped object ball (placed so the stripe is on the equator) in place of the cue ball. Illustration 34–35 depicts the side view of a short stop shot as compared to a follow shot. The sliding of the cue ball explains why stop shots are easier to execute on new, slippery cloth. On that slick surface, the cue ball slides more easily. On older cloth, the increased friction between the cloth and the cue ball makes it more likely that the cue ball will pick up forward roll rather than slide and stop.

Based on this explanation, we see why you cannot stop the cue ball precisely if you are stroking it too softly; such action causes it to pick up rotation almost immediately. This is because the cue ball has not been given enough energy to slide over the cloth. Thus, it is more susceptible to friction from the cloth. This will happen no matter where on the cue ball (center, low, or high) you strike. On the other hand, you do not want to get into the habit of slamming the balls into the pockets, even on stop shots. Stroking the balls too hard will cause your shots to rattle out of the pockets unless you have pocketed the ball absolutely cleanly. A good practice drill is to try to stop the cue ball, but at the slowest speed that still gets the job done.

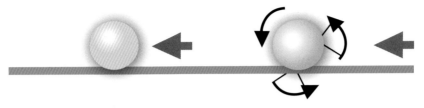

When you stroke the cue ball with follow, it rotates forward as it approaches the object ball.

On a short slop shot, however, the cue ball starts out with no forward roll and never picks up any. Instead, the cue ball slides across the cloth into the object ball.

Illustrations 34–35

• The Follow Shot •

Follow causes the cue ball to roll forward after hitting an object ball because the cue ball is rotating forward at the time it meets the object ball. In instances where the hit on the object ball is full and you want the cue ball to roll forward substantially after contact, the cue ball must be spinning forward faster at impact than for shots where less follow is desired. For most follow shots, you achieve forward rotation by stroking the cue ball north of its equator, and following through smoothly.

Using the same set-up shown in illustration 32, start by aiming the tip of your cue stick at the spot you normally would strike to achieve stop. Now, aim the tip of your cue stick *above* the spot you use for center. (You need not stray more than one tip's diameter from the center of the cue ball to achieve follow.) From this adjusted position, stroke the cue ball and, as always, follow through past the point of contact. The cue ball should follow forward across the table after contacting the object ball.

Many players fail to keep the cue stick level on their shots. In most cases, the player has raised the rear hand and strikes downward on the cue ball to a degree. Lowering the rear hand—adjusting what I call the "attitude" of the cue stick—will help you to follow the cue ball successfully if you tend to shoot downward on the cue ball.

Follow is a valuable tool at even the highest levels of the game. The best players realize that it is easier to gauge how far the cue ball will travel when using follow than when using draw, defined in the next section. Thus, you will notice that, in games like nine-ball—when players sometimes get the chance to place the cue ball anywhere on the table they like ("ball-in-hand," as it is commonly called)—they often choose to place the cue ball in a spot allowing them to follow the cue ball, rather than choosing a position where draw is needed.

Practice by setting up a shot such as the one shown in illustration 36, and then try to follow the cue ball to different points on the table. Start with closer targets and, after gaining a sense of how to follow to these closer targets, try to follow the cue ball to points further and further down the table.

It is to your advantage to be able to follow forcefully, which will allow you to follow the length of the table or off of a rail. A powerful follow stroke also allows you to separate a large cluster of balls to free object balls for additional shots. More important, however, is to develop a follow stroke that you can count on to deliver you to specific points on the table. Better players stroke the follow shot so that the cue ball does not travel all that fast, but can continue to roll a long distance. The key is the smooth follow-through critical to all types of shots.

Don't forget to apply to your follow stroke what we learned from our discussion of the short stop stroke! On delicate follow shots, the best speed may be to stroke the cue ball softly, since the cue ball will pick up forward rotation on its own. Similarly, as the distance between the cue ball and the object ball lengthens, it becomes less and less necessary to stroke the cue ball high to achieve

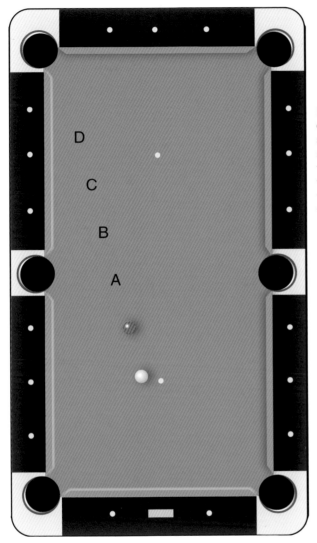

Practice following the cue ball to different spots on the table, starting with closer targets (A and B) and then trying to follow with control to further targets on the table (C and D).

Illustration 36

follow. The distance the cue ball travels before reaching the object ball allows the cue ball to pick up forward rotation from the cloth with just a center-ball hit. This allows you to achieve follow on longer shots by contacting the cue ball at its equator, your most reliable target on the cue ball.

• The Draw Shot •

Learning to cause the cue ball to reverse direction, or draw, after it makes contact with the object ball is one of the most pleasing accomplishments for the player just starting out. Even after years of playing, veteran players get a nice feeling when they have stroked the cue ball so that it draws back to the perfect position for the next shot.

With draw, the cue ball is spinning backward at the moment of impact with the object ball. On straight-in shots, the reverse rotation on the cue ball "draws" the cue ball backwards after the object ball has been driven forward by the impact. On angled shots, draw will not make the cue ball retreat straight back, but still influences the path of the cue ball, as discussed in chapter 6.

Although drawing the cue ball does not come naturally to every player, everyone can learn to do it. Let's say that the balls are once again in the position shown in illustration 32. We start with our reference point: aiming the cue stick at the center of the cue ball as if we're going to hit and stop. Now, instead of lowering the rear hand and raising the tip of the cue, as we did when we applied follow to the cue ball, we *lower* the tip of the cue stick. Take your practice strokes with the cue stick in this position. Now we're ready to make the actual stroke, but it is again important, as always, to stroke through the point of contact.

Forcing the cue ball to reverse its tracks and head backwards after contact confounds many new players. Getting the cue ball to draw enough can sometimes be accomplished by simply contacting the cue ball lower. If the cue ball still does not draw back, there are techniques to keep in mind that will help you to draw the cue ball consistently. Keep your draw stroke accurate, smooth, and fluid by keeping your head and body down throughout the shot, and making sure that your rear hand is not gripping the cue stick too tightly.

For me, a certain mental image has helped to produce draw. When drawing the cue ball, I think about bringing my rear hand to an immediate and sudden stop *after* following through the point of contact. Some players look as if they are dragging their cue stick through the stroke when they try to draw. Drawing the cue ball requires a precise hit and a smooth stroke, neither of which is achieved through a lazy stroke—even when the cue ball is struck below center. The usual result of dragging the cue stick through the stroke is that the cue ball does not draw as much as the player intended; the cue ball will not retreat enough, or what should be draw ends up as a stop shot. Instead, think of accelerating the cue stick through the point of contact, following through, and then bringing the rear hand to a sharp stop. Other players may have their own mental imagery to achieve draw. From my experience, if you follow the above steps, the cue ball will draw.

• The Long Stop Shot •

Stop shots become trickier as the distance between the cue ball and the object ball lengthens. On longer shots, stroking the cue ball at its center will not stop the cue ball because, although the cue ball starts out by sliding across the cloth, by the time it reaches the object ball, it has picked up forward rotation from the friction of the cloth. Take a striped object ball and, once again, use it in place of the cue ball. This time, however, set up a longer (but still straight-in) shot. With your striped "cue ball," you can see how forward slide becomes forward roll.

Going back to how a stop shot works, we remember that the cue ball must stop on a straight-in shot when, at impact, the cue ball is free of any forward or reverse rotation. Keeping this in mind, we can successfully stop the cue ball on longer shots by applying reverse spin, or draw, to the cue ball so that—just at the instant it reaches the object ball—the cue ball is not spinning forward or in reverse. Applying just the right amount of draw to the cue ball to make it stop on a long, straight-in shot calls for a keen sense of touch . . . and practice. Using a striped ball as a cue ball allows you to see how what starts out as draw becomes forward roll. You'll see that for an instant in between, the ball is neither in reverse nor forward rotation. Adjusting the amount of draw needed, depending upon the length of the shot, is crucial. For longer shots, more draw is needed; for shorter shots, less draw will do. Each player is different when it comes to stopping the cue ball on long shots. The only way to figure out precisely how low to address the cue ball and how hard you'll need to stroke it is to experiment and practice on the table.

• The Essentials •

1. On *all* shots, follow through past the point of contact.

2. On short stop shots, stroke the cue ball firmly enough for the cue ball to slide across the cloth when you apply a center-ball hit.

3. For follow, adjust the "attitude" of your cue by lowering the rear hand slightly, and aiming the tip of the cue above the center of the cue ball.

4. For draw, lower the tip of your cue, and stroke through the cue ball below its center.

5. If you are not drawing the cue ball consistently or you're not getting enough draw, lower the cue tip further and make sure you are following through.

CHAPTER

6

Moving the Cue Ball Successfully

Being able to stop the cue ball, or move it back or forward, on straight-in shots is a must. Sometimes, you'll be fortunate enough to be able to play a series of shots that only require stop, which is ideal. Unless you're lucky enough to start your inning with a layout that allows you to play only stop-shot position, however, you should want to have an angle on your shots. Avoiding straight-in shots gives you the most flexibility in terms of getting the cue ball into a position for your next shot.

In illustration 37, we see two shots on the table. Shot A is a straight-in shot, making it difficult to move the cue ball to different locations on the table other than straight forward or straight back. Shot B is angled and will allow you, once you know how, to move the cue ball to virtually any location on the table. The easiest way to start thinking about how to move the cue ball off a shot such as shot B is to first figure out where the cue ball will tend to go, simply based on where the cue ball meets the object ball, (where the cue ball will travel naturally). The key to where the cue ball will travel naturally is the tangent line.

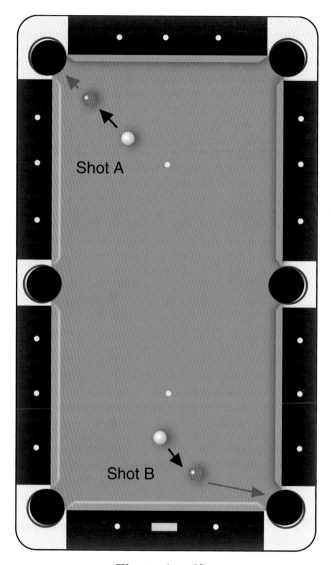

Shot A

Shot B

Illustration 37

• The Tangent Line and the Natural Path of the Cue Ball •

The tangent line is the line that splits between the cue ball and the object ball at the moment those two balls meet. Put another way, the tangent line is perpendicular to the line connecting the centers of the cue ball and the object ball at the moment they meet (illustration 38).

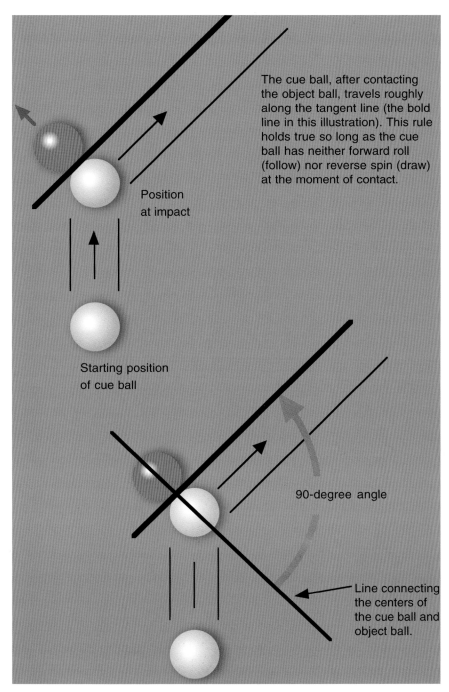

The cue ball, after contacting the object ball, travels roughly along the tangent line (the bold line in this illustration). This rule holds true so long as the cue ball has neither forward roll (follow) nor reverse spin (draw) at the moment of contact.

Position at impact

Starting position of cue ball

90-degree angle

Line connecting the centers of the cue ball and object ball.

Illustration 38

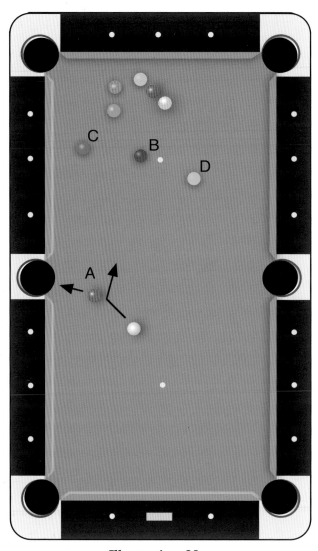

Illustration 38a

Now take a look at illustration 38A. It is easy to see that when you pocket ball A, the cue ball will travel down towards the foot of the table in the general direction of the other object balls. You can learn to understand—and *control*—where the cue ball will travel. If you shoot at A in the same manner you would shoot to stop the cue ball on a straight-in shot, the cue ball will naturally travel towards ball B. You can also make the cue ball move so that it travels towards ball C, ahead of the natural path of the cue ball, or towards ball D, behind the natural path, as explained later in this chapter.

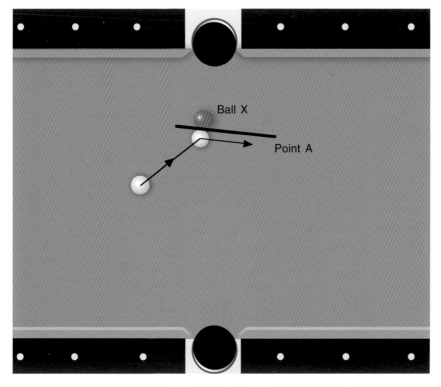

Illustration 39

We will first focus on causing the cue ball to travel roughly along the tangent line. You will accomplish this if the cue ball, at the moment it contacts the object ball, has neither forward nor reverse spin (neither follow nor draw). You can test out how well this works on the table. In illustration 39, the tangent line indicates that the cue ball will head towards Point A after it contacts object ball X, so long as the cue ball does not have any follow or draw at the moment it meets object Ball X. Now for the test: Before pocketing X, place another object ball (Ball Y) on Point A; then stroke the cue ball into Ball X using the same type of stroke you would use to stop the cue ball. If you make the shot and succeed in avoiding unintentional follow or draw on the cue ball, the cue ball will run right into Ball Y.

Let's look at some examples of position play using the tangent line. In illustration 40, the goal is to pocket Ball X and play position for Ball Y. The tangent line tells us that if we pocket ball X with a center-ball hit and the proper speed, the cue ball will travel approximately straight down the table to the spot marked A, which leaves us in perfect position for Ball Y—without the need to force the cue ball to move into position using excessive draw, follow, or english. This is known as "natural" position, since we achieve position by merely allowing the cue ball to travel in the direction it was tending to go in any event, just by virtue of where the cue ball made contact with Ball X.

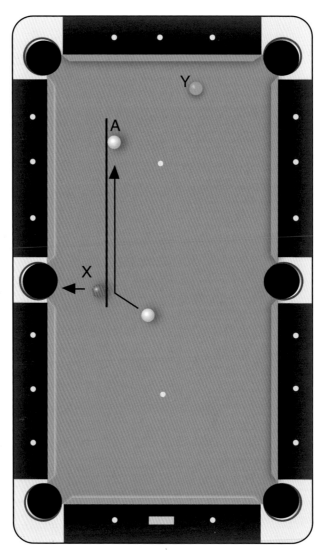

Illustration 40

Illustration 41 shows another example of natural position, this time involving one rail. Here, the tangent line tells us that after we stroke the cue ball with center, it will contact Ball X such that the cue ball will head almost straight into the rail, towards Point A. Since the cue ball is rolling almost straight into the rail, it will roll almost straight out (see p. 88), towards Point B for position on Ball Y.

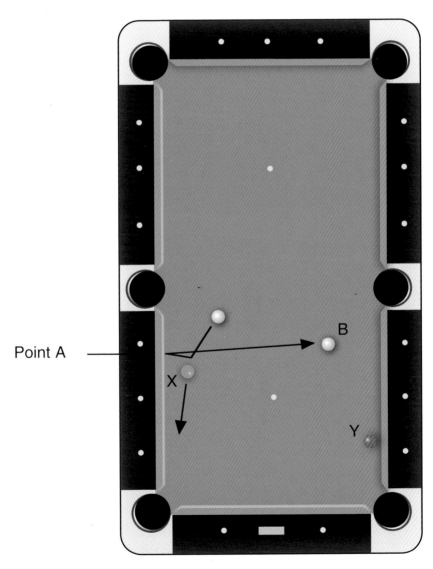

Illustration 41

• Speed Control •

The only requirement for moving the cue ball successfully on natural position shots—other than pocketing the object ball without applying spin to the cue ball accidentally—is to stroke the cue ball with the proper speed. Speed control is vital for every type of shot except stop shots; and a lot of playing pool well at any level is controlling the speed of the cue ball.

Speed control develops with practice. That simple notion, however, does not specify how a player can develop that control as quickly as possible, and how a player can summon whatever speed control he or she has when it's needed most—in a competitive game.

There are two potential problems with controlling speed: misjudging how much speed you *should* apply, and applying more or less speed than you intend. You can avoid these problems if, before getting down into your shooting stance, you first decide how hard or softly you want to stroke the cue ball. Do not make this decision after you are already in your stance and taking your practice strokes. Do not change this decision as you are just about to shoot, either. If you have a change of heart at any time after you are already in your stance, simply stand up, and think it over again.

To judge how much speed to apply, look at how much of the object ball the cue ball will be hitting when those two balls make contact. You may have a straight-in shot or a nearly straight-in shot, (i.e., a "full" hit). Other times you will have a "thin" hit (or cut); that is, your cue ball will not be running into much of the object ball. On extremely thin hits, the cue ball merely grazes the edge of the object ball.

Many players, even intermediate ones, look only at how far the cue ball will need to travel. They ignore how thick or thin the hit will be. When faced with a situation where the cue ball will have to travel across or around the table, these players always stroke the cue ball too hard. As a result, the cue ball rolls past its target. You can avoid making these types of mistakes by keeping in mind the following: On a thin hit, very little of the cue ball's energy is absorbed by the object ball. For this reason, the cue ball has plenty left over after contacting the object ball, and thus will roll a good distance even if the stroke applied is not very forceful. On these thin hits, the cue ball needs less energy at the start in order to get it to where it needs to be for your next shot. Stroke these shots with a delicate touch. (The only time you'll need to stroke these shots with more force is when the cut on the object ball is so thin that you will need to speed up the cue ball just to make sure that it transfers enough energy to the object ball, to allow the object ball to reach the pocket. This scenario will not come up very often.) However, on thick hits, much of the cue ball's energy is absorbed at impact by the object ball. If you need to make the cue ball travel a fair distance off of a thick hit, you will always need more speed than would be applied on a thinner cut.

Let's say that you have developed a keen sense of how much speed should be applied to particular shots based on the thickness of the hit. Your judgment, as far as how much speed should be applied to the cue ball, is sound. How can you make sure that you apply the amount of speed you intend? No one is perfect in this department. All players over-hit or under-hit shots. The better players simply do so less often, and recover from their position errors better and more frequently.

Advanced players visualize the desired result before they stroke the cue ball. Seeing, within your mind, the cue ball floating over to the ideal position for your next shot works wonders. Before making contact with the cue ball, you should also think about how it feels to stroke the cue ball with the perfect speed. You should even become sensitive to what it sounds like when your cue stick makes a perfect hit on the cue ball.

Besides these mental techniques, you may consider other ways to control cue ball speed. Some players will shorten the distance between their bridge hand and the cue ball when they must stroke the cue ball softly, to help ensure that they won't overpower the cue ball. When you need a more forceful stroke, lengthening the space between your bridge hand and the cue ball helps to guarantee that you stroke the cue ball with enough power. An extreme example of the application of this concept is when you break the balls at the start of a nine-ball or eight-ball game. All top players lengthen their bridges on these types of power break shots. So should you.

Another technique to control speed is to take your practice strokes the same way you intend to deliver your actual stroke. It is difficult to caress the cue ball delicately after vigorously sawing the cue

stick back and forth on your practice strokes. You can use your practice strokes to acclimate yourself to how you intend to actually execute
the stroke. Many players take their practice strokes at the same moderate speed no matter how hard or softly they will be delivering the
actual stroke, relying solely on mental planning and imagery to prepare for delivery of the stroke at the proper speed. Experiment with
both methods to find out what works best for you.

• Controlling Your Destiny—How To Alter the Natural Path of the Cue Ball •

It's often possible to play position off of angled shots using only natural position and speed control. You can refine your position play,
however, by altering the natural path of the cue ball through the
use of follow and draw. Refer again to illustration 38A. It is follow
that allows you to direct the cue ball ahead of its natural path, towards ball C. It is draw that allows you to direct the cue ball behind
its natural path, towards ball D.

In illustration 42, you could achieve position on ball B with a
center-ball hit on the cue ball. With center ball, the cue ball ends
up at point X, as shown in the illustration, for a reasonable shot on
ball B. It would be better still, however, if you could somehow position the cue ball closer to ball B. That would occur if you could
cause the cue ball to roll ahead of the natural tangent line to end
up closer to point Y.

What causes the cue ball to roll ahead of the tangent line? Follow. If you stroke the cue ball above center, applying follow to the
cue ball, it will be spinning forward at contact. This added spin will
cause it to travel ahead of the 90-degree tangent line, towards point
Y, and will leave you with a better shot on ball B. This route is shown
by the bold line in illustration 43. You can see from the bold line
that the cue ball starts out by skidding along the tangent line (towards point X) before the forward rotation on the cue ball takes
over—from friction with the cloth—causing the cue ball to travel
ahead of the tangent line.

Notice that no side-spin (english) is necessary. Thus, applying
follow does not make pocketing your shot any more difficult, since

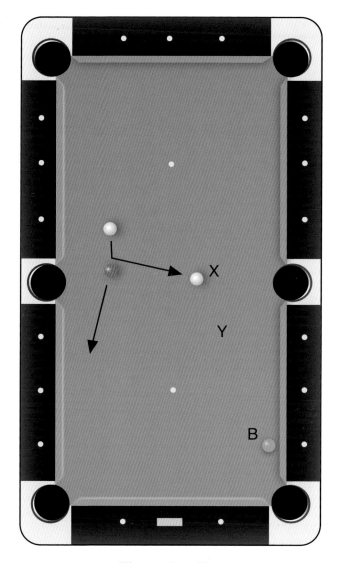

Illustration 42

aiming adjustments that must be made when you stroke the cue ball with english don't apply. (English is discussed in chapter 7.) The only difference is superior position. As a bonus, applying follow in this situation completely eliminates any risk of a scratch into the side pocket marked Z.

By stroking the cue ball with more speed, the cue ball skids along the 90-degree tangent line longer before the cue ball follows

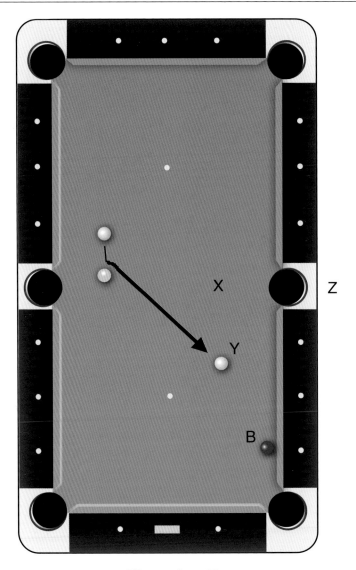

Illustration 43

forward. With a softer stroke, the cue ball skids along the tangent line a shorter distance before its forward rotation sends it ahead of the tangent line.

Let's look at another example. In illustration 44, you could once again use center ball to obtain position on your next shot (ball B). With good speed control you could end up at point A with a center-ball hit, but that leaves you with a fairly long shot on ball B, and more angle on the shot than most players would want. You

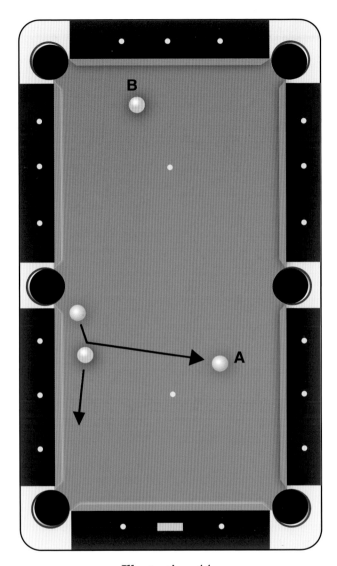

Illustration 44

would be better off if you could somehow cause the cue ball to travel *behind* the 90-degree tangent line.

Causing the cue ball to travel backwards on a straight-in shot calls for draw. On angled shots, when you want the cue ball to travel behind the natural position path along the tangent line, draw is again the answer. Illustration 45 shows what happens when you apply draw to the cue ball: It retreats from the natural path and leaves you in far better position to take care of ball B next. Simple.

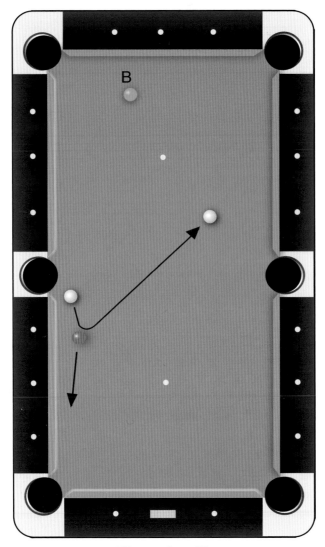

Illustration 45

• Playing Position Off a Rail •

You can also use draw and follow when playing position off a rail. First, let's consider how the cue ball or an object ball bounces off a rail. In general, the wider the angle at which a ball approaches a rail, the wider the angle it takes when it departs the rail; and the narrower the angle at which a ball approaches a rail, the narrower the angle it takes after it contacts the rail. As a rough approximation, the incoming angle equals the outgoing angle, but that rough

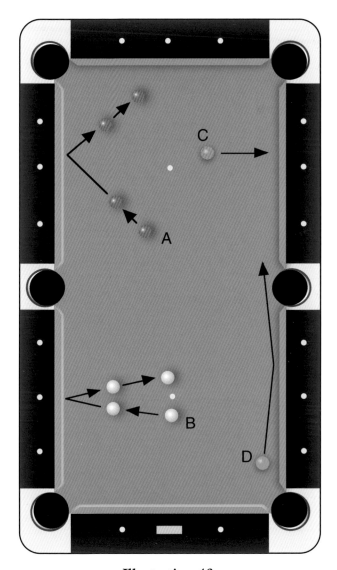

Illustration 46

rule relies on the speed applied to the shot, whether or not english is applied, and characteristics of the particular table on which you are playing. Illustration 46 shows ball A approaching the rail at a wider angle than ball B, and the direction the balls take off the rail (assuming in both cases a medium speed and no english). You can remember this effect intuitively by thinking of the most extreme examples. When you stroke a ball straight into a rail (as shown by ball C in illustration 46), you expect it to come straight back (i.e., the angle is zero). If you stroke the cue ball so that it barely contacts the rail, it will not come straight back towards you but will instead travel away from you at a very wide angle (ball D in illustration 46).

Another general rule is that the faster a ball is moving when it contacts the rail, the narrower the angle at which the ball leaves the rail, because the ball sinks further into the cushion. For this reason, you can stroke a ball into the exact same spot on the rail at the exact same angle, and alter the angle at which the ball leaves the rail by using only speed (i.e., without any english). In illustration 47, the ball

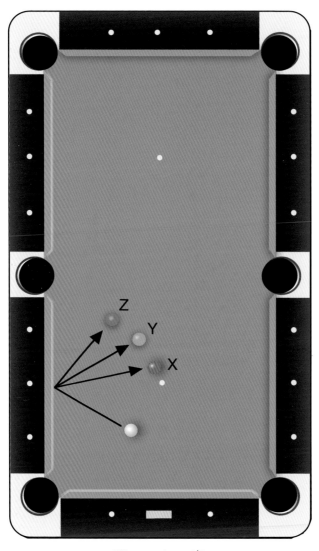

Illustration 47

is starting from the same place and hitting the same spot on the rail, but it is leaving the rail at three different angles because it was struck at three different speeds, ranging from X (the fastest) to Z (the slowest), with Y being struck at a speed in between.

Now let's take a look at playing position off a rail, starting with illustration 48. Here, you can end up with a shot on ball B by simply stroking the cue ball with a center ball. With center ball, the cue ball travels along the tangent line to point X on the rail and banks

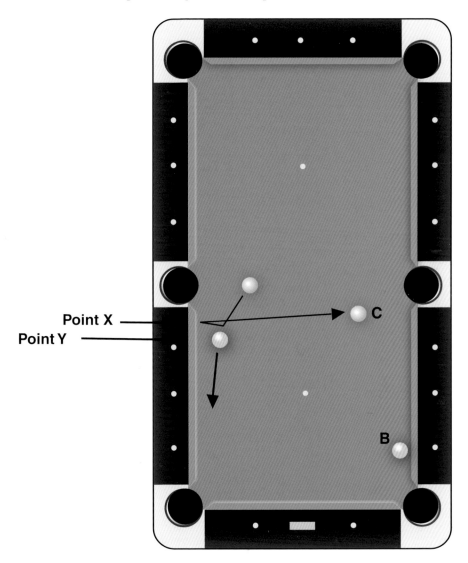

Illustration 48

across the table as shown, ending up at C. If you could cause the cue ball to contact the rail at point Y, however, you could improve on your position and end up closer to ball B.

Since you want the cue ball to travel ahead of the natural path dictated by the tangent line, you'll need follow. Follow will take the cue ball to point H as shown by the bold line in illustration 49. Again, you won't need any right or left english. All you'll need is follow.

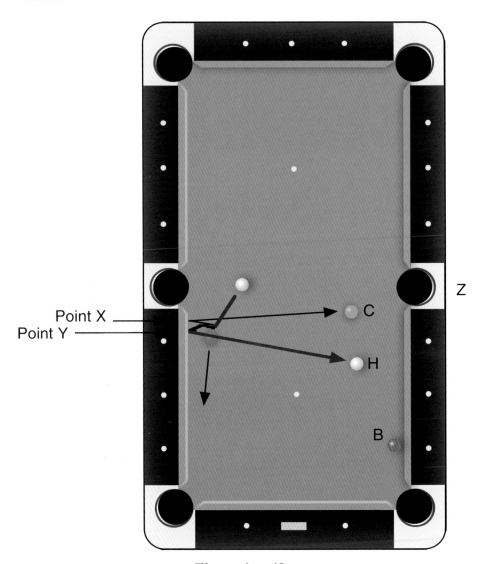

Illustration 49

In illustration 50, the same center ball hit you applied in illustration 48 will yield fair position on ball B. If you could get the cue ball to retreat from its natural path and contact the rail closer to the side pocket, however, your position on ball B would improve. Since you want the cue ball to travel behind its natural path, you must apply draw. With draw, you will send the cue ball on the path shown in illustration 51. The result is superior position on ball B.

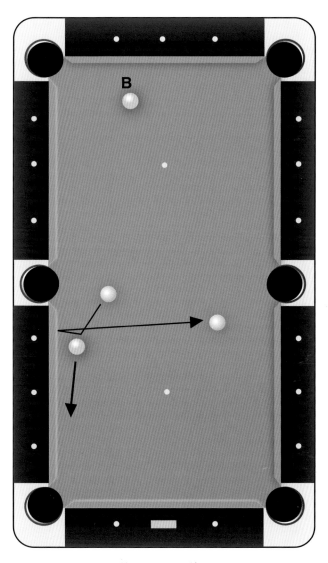

Illustration 50

By maintaining an angle on your shots, and considering how the cue ball will travel naturally, you will develop the ability to play position for most shots using natural position (a center-ball hit) or follow or draw.

Let's review the essentials of moving the cue ball successfully off of angled shots.

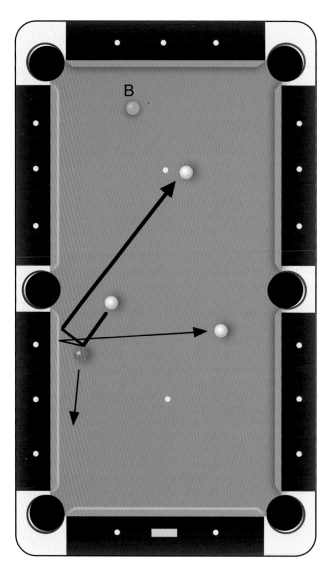

Illustration 51

• The Essentials •

1. First, figure out the tangent line; that is, where the cue ball will travel naturally with a center-ball hit.

2. Think about whether you can achieve satisfactory position using center ball and the right speed control.

3. Consider whether you can improve on natural position by causing the cue ball to travel ahead of the tangent line (using follow), or behind the tangent line (using draw).

4. After you decide whether you'll be using center, follow, or draw, think about how much speed you'll need to apply, bearing in mind how thick or thin your hit on the object ball will be.

5. After thinking through the above steps, get down into your shooting stance, take your practice strokes, and finally, let the stroke go.

"English" as a Second Language— Understanding and Applying Side-Spin

nglish is the spin imparted to the cue ball when it is stroked to the left or right of center—in other words, side-spin. Just as the friction created by follow and draw affects how the cue ball behaves, the friction created as the cue ball spins like a top on the cloth alters the cue ball's path.

Probably the quickest way to progress in pool is to avoid using any english until you have a thorough understanding of and comfort with how to stand, how to stroke the cue ball, how to pocket balls, and how to play position using stop, follow, and draw. Many a player has regressed in ability due to the tendency to use english improperly or excessively. Even at the top levels of play, many position shots can be made without any english. Stop, follow, and draw are often enough. Being mindful that english can create havoc, when a professional pool player absolutely needs to pocket a shot and wants to "cinch" it, he or she will often do so by minimizing or avoiding english on the shot. To become a competent and complete player, however, you will need to master english.

• Understanding English •

If your game has reached the point where you can pocket shots and play stop-shot, follow, and draw position with some consistency, then it is time to add english to your arsenal. Applying english successfully starts with a solid bridge. Since you will be making finely calibrated adjustments to how far off center you stroke the cue ball, it is important that you can count on your bridge to remain perfectly still throughout the stroke, and tight enough to focus the tip on the desired target on the cue ball. For this reason, you may find yourself feeling more secure applying english using a closed bridge rather than an open one.

When using english, it is also important to avoid stroking the cue ball too far away from its center. A common recommendation is to keep the tip of the cue stick within one cue tip's width of the center of the cue ball. By doing so, you reduce the chance of mis-hitting the cue ball (miscuing) and improve your chances of controlling your english.

How far off center you stroke the cue ball influences how much english will be applied. The further off center you stroke the cue ball, the more english you will achieve, but also, as noted above, the more risk you take that you will miscue your shot. While it is better to stay near the center of the cue ball when applying english, you should experiment in practice with how far off center you can stroke the cue ball while maintaining control, so you'll have the skills for those situations when you absolutely need them.

Controlling english is no easy task. Let's start by looking at the effects of english. When you stroke the cue ball to the right of center, the cue ball does not roll straight ahead. Instead, the cue ball first moves to the left, an effect called "squirt" or "deflection." The cue ball will then tend to curve slightly to the right, especially if the butt of the cue is elevated. Provided the cue ball is still spinning when it reaches the object ball, the spin you imparted to the cue ball (right english) will cause the object ball to head further in the opposite direction (towards the left) than if no english had been used. This effect is called "throw." Thus, right english on the cue ball throws the object ball to the left, and left english on the cue ball throws the object ball to the right.

One way to remember this effect is to think of the gears of a machine. English reverses direction between the cue ball and an object ball just as a gear spinning in one direction causes the gear next to it to spin in the opposite direction (illustration 51A).

Gaining the power to cause the balls to spin, curve, and throw surely expands your possibilities on a pool table. Remember, however, that what causes english to create these effects is friction. This means that *any factor that affects friction will affect how english reacts on the cue ball and on the object ball.*

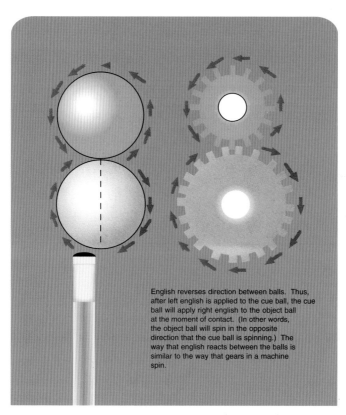

English reverses direction between balls. Thus, after left english is applied to the cue ball, the cue ball will apply right english to the object ball at the moment of contact. (In other words, the object ball will spin in the opposite direction that the cue ball is spinning.) The way that english reacts between the balls is similar to the way that gears in a machine spin.

Illustration 51a

Many factors affect friction. The most important factor to keep in mind when it comes to the throw effect is speed. Thus, when you need to throw an object ball a lot, you must stroke the cue ball softly. This concept confuses some people, who expect to spin the cue ball faster and throw the object ball further the harder they stroke the cue ball. In reality, the opposite is true. For maximum throw, use minimum speed.

When calculating how much english to apply, you must also factor in the distance the cue ball will travel until it reaches the object ball. The further the distance, the more the curve effect on the cue ball will impact your effort to send it to the proper contact point on the object ball. Also, if the cue ball must travel a long distance before it reaches the object ball, the cue ball will be transferring less spin (or no spin) to the object ball by the time it finally gets there.

Playing conditions that affect friction will also affect how much english will impact your shots. The condition of the balls, for example, will affect english. If the balls have not been cleaned and the friction between the cue ball and the object balls is accentuated, the throw effect will be accentuated as well. Trying to sort out the various effects of deflection, curve, and throw—while factoring in the variables created by the playing conditions—is not easy, and should give you a sense of why applying any english at all is a risky proposition. If you are able to eliminate all of these variables by shooting a shot without english, it's a good idea. When you must apply english, pay attention to how much the english is "taking" on that given day. One tip's width of english on a one-foot shot may create a far different effect on any given day from the next. It is up to you to make adjustments based on the conditions. Only through practice and playing will you be able to learn what types of adjustments are necessary.

• Applying English •

Let's look at an example of applying english. In illustration 52, you are about to pocket the object ball into the corner pocket. Bear in mind that you need not apply any english to pocket this shot. Moreover, your chances of pocketing the ball improve if you choose to play the shot without any english. At the same time, in this example, you may choose to apply right english to this shot in order to cause

Cushion A

Cushion B

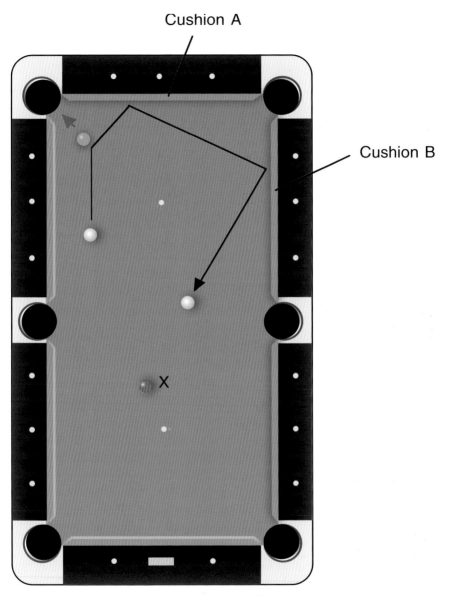

Illustration 52

the cue ball to spin (or "run") off cushions A and B so you can achieve position on ball X.

Right english will cause the cue ball to deflect to the left. If deflection were the only effect created by application of english, and you aimed this shot the same way you aimed with no english, then applying right english would cause you to hit the object ball too full and you would undercut the shot. Curve and throw, however, also come into play. Right english will tend to cause the cue ball to curve somewhat to the right. (You should generally keep your cue as level as possible through the stroke to try to minimize this curve effect.) The right english you apply to the cue ball will also throw the object ball to the left after contact. Thus, the combined effects of curve and throw, in this example, tend to cause the cue ball to move to the right and the object ball to move to the left—in sum, both the curve and throw effects will cause you to overcut the shot if you aimed the shot the same way you might aim without any english.

Considering these effects, we see that when applying english on the opposite side of the direction in which we are cutting the object ball and at a slow speed (which maximizes the effect of throw), we will need to cut the shot less. Applying english on the opposite side of the direction in which you are cutting the object ball is known as "outside" english.

In illustration 52, since we are applying outside english (right english to a shot where the object ball is being cut to the left), we must aim the cue ball for a fuller hit on the object ball than if we were stroking the shot without english. If you hit this particular shot with right english and slowly enough, you might be able to pocket the object ball by aiming the cue ball straight at the center of the object ball.

Looking again at illustration 52, let's consider the effects of applying left english. With left english on the cue ball, it will deflect to the right and then curve to the left before it reaches the object ball. The left english on the cue ball will throw the object ball to the right. That means that, assuming a slow speed and minimal deflection, left english on this shot will tend to cause the shot to be undercut. Applying english on the same side in which you are cutting the ball is called "inside" english. When applying inside english at slow speeds, you must aim to cut the shot more than you would when using a center-ball hit.

The throw effect can be substantial. Take a look at illustration 53. In that illustration, the cue ball and object ball are touching ("frozen") so that they are aligned with the upper left corner pocket. Since right english will throw the object ball to the left, you can observe the effects of throw by applying right english to the cue

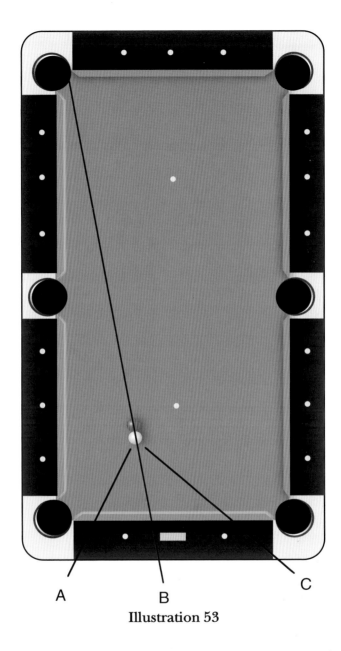

A   B   C

Illustration 53

ball. This can be done in two different ways: One way is to stroke the cue ball straight ahead—aligning your cue stick with line B—and striking the cue ball to the right of center. Another way is to align your cue stick with line C, and stroking the cue ball at its center. Either way, you will throw the object ball to the left.

You will be able to throw object balls enough to pocket balls that do not look like they can be made, and, unfortunately, miss shots that look unmissable. Going back to illustration 53, by stroking the cue ball along line C at a slow speed, you will throw the object ball enough to the left to miss the shot on the left side of the corner pocket. Stroking the same exact shot from line A will cause the object ball to be thrown to the right of the pocket. Shooting from line B with a center-ball hit will sink the object ball. You can get these three different results from the same starting position, all depending upon the effects of throw!

In illustration 54, the cue ball and the object ball, ball Y, are not aligned with the pocket. Instead, ball Y is aimed to the right of the pocket as shown by the dotted line. You can still pocket ball Y, however, using throw. You obviously need to throw ball Y to the left. Since english reverses itself between balls, use right english to throw the object ball to the left and into the pocket.

In illustration 55, two object balls are frozen together rather than an object ball and the cue ball. The object balls are aligned with the pocket. If the cue ball is in location B, all you need to do to pocket ball Z is to stroke the cue ball straight into ball Y, at the contact point shown. If you're starting from point A or point C, however, you cannot simply aim the cue ball straight into ball Y, since you will throw Z off line. Instead, from either of these positions, you must aim so the cue ball contacts Y at the contact point shown.

You may find yourself stuck in a position, however, where you can only contact the right side of ball Y because other object balls are in the way. You may still be able to pocket ball Z—despite the throw effect—by hitting ball Y with a lot of speed. Stroking this shot hard will minimize the throw, and, if the pocket is big enough, you'll make the shot without hitting ball Y at the ideal contact point.

The same principles apply when three object balls are frozen, as shown in illustration 56. In that illustration, balls X and Y are aligned to the right of the pocket (as shown by the dotted line), and ball Z is positioned so that it will be applying right english to ball Y. If you hit ball Z into ball Y, the right english will throw ball X in the opposite direction—to the left—and into the corner pocket, as shown by the solid line.

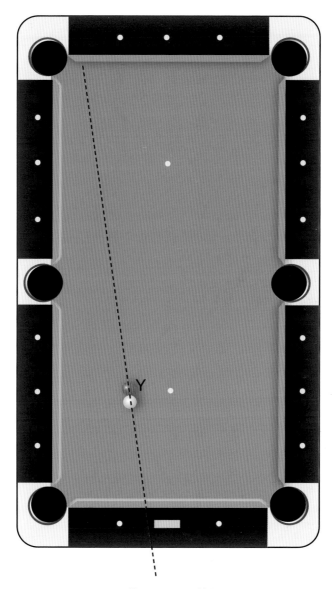

Illustration 54

In illustration 57, balls X and Y are in the same position as in the prior illustration. The difference is that ball Z is frozen on the other side of the other two balls and will apply left english to ball Y. Here, hitting ball Z into ball Y cannot succeed, since the left english applied to ball Y will throw ball X to the right—and even

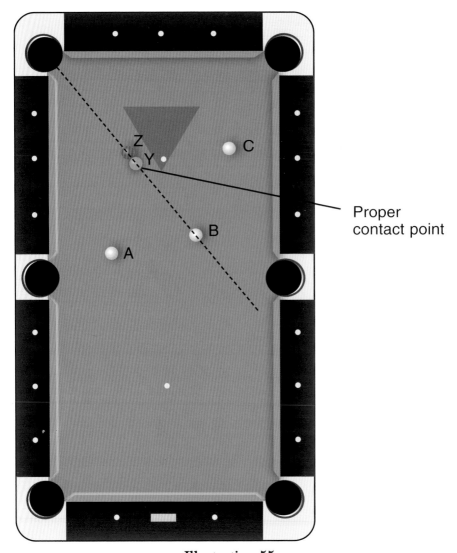

Proper
contact point

Illustration 55

further from the pocket—as illustrated by the solid line in illustration 57.

Sometimes you will hear the terms "running" and "reverse" english. These terms, like outside and inside english, indicate which side of the cue ball is being struck, depending on the direction the cue ball is headed in. Running and reverse english, however, occur only in instances in which the cue ball strikes a rail. Running english widens the angle between the path of the cue ball to

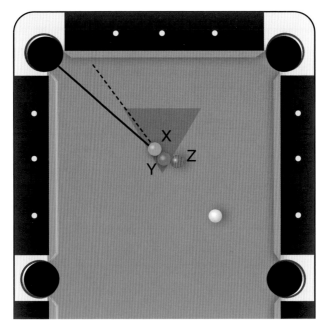

Illustration 56

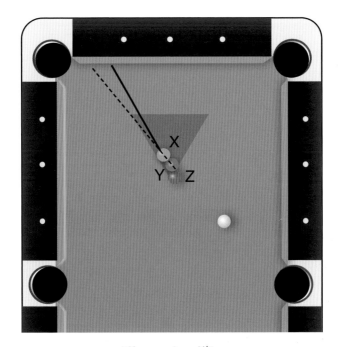

Illustration 57

the rail and the path of the cue ball after it leaves the rail. Reverse, or "hold-up," english has the opposite effect.

Take a look at illustration 58. The black line shows the path of the cue ball when it is stroked with center ball. When running english is applied (right english in this illustration), the cue ball is spinning in the same direction from which it leaves the cushion, and thus the cue ball leaves the cushion at a wider angle, as shown by the dark gray line in the illustration. Reverse (left) english has the opposite effect. With reverse, the cue ball is spinning in the opposite direction from the direction in which the cue ball is coming off the cushion, narrowing the angle at which the cue ball leaves the cushion, as shown by the light gray line in illustration 58.

English is most commonly used to control the cue ball in some fashion, causing it to move a certain way or, in some instances, to

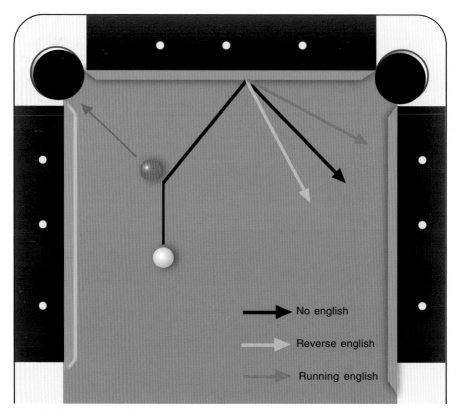

No english

Reverse english

Running english

Illustration 58

move less or not at all. Refer back to illustration 49 in Chapter 6. In that illustration, you could play position on ball B using less follow by also applying inside (left) english. The left english will help to send the cue ball towards point H for your next shot rather than point C.

Looking back to illustration 51, you could achieve position with less draw by also applying running (right) english. From the position shown in that illustration, try stroking the cue ball at 5:00 instead of 6:00. Doing so will mean applying less draw since you won't be stroking the cue ball as low. You will be adding right english, however, since you will be contacting the cue ball to the right of center. You will see that the right english widens the angle off of the rail for easier position on ball B. Using english in this manner is a common example of how all accomplished players apply english to certain shots. No matter how many professionals and book writers advocate minimizing english, in practice, probably all of them would apply right english to the draw shot depicted in illustration 51.

Sometimes english is helpful when used to prevent the cue ball from moving too much. In illustration 59, you're playing nine-ball, in which the lowest-numbered ball on the table must be the first to be contacted by the cue ball. You are left with a slightly angled shot on the eight ball in the side pocket. If you had landed straight on the eight ball, you would have achieved perfect position since, from such a lie, you could simply stop the cue ball on the eight for position on the nine in the corner. Because you're at an angle, if you shoot with center, the cue ball will head too far up table for a satisfactory shot on the nine, as depicted by the gray line in the illustration. You may even roll far enough to end up at position X, leaving a poor shot (or no shot) on the nine ball. By applying right (outside) english to the cue ball, however, you will be able to make a fuller hit on the eight ball. Instead of cutting the eight into the side pocket, you will be throwing the eight ball to the left and into the pocket. The fuller hit on the eight means the cue ball moves less after contact, as shown by the black line and position Y in illustration 59, allowing you to keep the cue ball closer to the vicinity of the eight ball after the shot, for position on the nine.

Running english is commonly used to spin the cue ball off two rails to return to the center of the table for position. In illustration

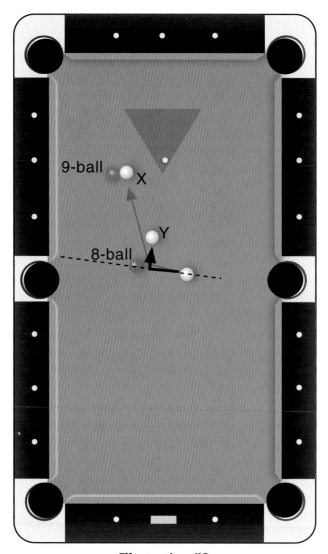

Illustration 59

60, you're shooting at ball A and looking to get the cue ball to the shaded area for a shot on ball B or ball C into the same corner pocket. By applying running (right) english, the cue ball will spin naturally off the foot rail, the right side rail, and into the desired position.

Although avoiding english is the general rule, in this example it is better to use english. If you were to attempt the same shot

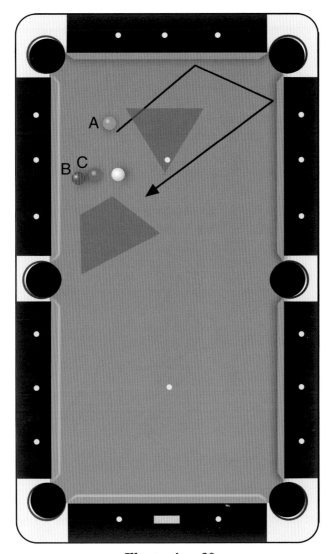

Illustration 60

without any english, more force would be required to move the cue ball to the desired area. Forcing the cue ball in that way will tend to make you miss the shot completely since you will be required to hit the shot with a lot of speed. Here, english simplifies—rather than complicates—matters.

• The Essentials •

1. Apply english only when necessary.

2. When applying english, apply the least amount necessary. Keep the tip of the cue within a tip's diameter of the center of the cue ball whenever possible.

3. Remember that english reverses itself between balls. Right english applied to the cue ball will throw an object ball to the left.

4. With outside english, you will generally need to aim for a fuller hit on the object ball. With inside english, you should generally aim for a thinner hit.

5. Running english will widen the angle the cue ball takes after it leaves a rail. Reverse english will narrow that angle.

When Worlds Collide (And When You Should Make Sure They Don't)

Running countless balls would be much easier if the balls always arranged themselves so that each one would be available for a clear shot, with no messy knots of balls cluttering up the layout of the table. Then all you'd need to do is pick off the shots one by one, and move the cue ball successfully from one shot to the next. In reality, the game does not offer such easy solutions. Succeeding at pool requires a player to think ahead, and to exercise enough control over the cue ball to pocket balls, move from shot to shot, *and* separate clusters of balls when the need arises.

While the need to separate clusters complicates an already difficult game, it also offers opportunity. One of the best feelings in pool is to watch the cue ball pocket your shot and then continue on to take apart a cluster, leaving you with another shot (and a chance to run out the rest of the table without any further problems). The feeling of controlling all of the balls on the table in this fashion can be breathtaking—like converting a split in bowling or blasting a golf ball out of a sand trap to within a few inches from the cup.

When it comes to separating clusters, you must first consider how hard you will need to stroke the cue ball in order to get the job done. The idea is not to crash into every cluster, scattering the balls in every direction. Doing so may seem fun at first, but you will lose control of the cue ball and risk scratching the cue ball into a pocket. Not only that, but the balls driven from the cluster will be thrown to the far corners of the table, leaving you with longer shots and more distance to travel between shots.

On the other hand, stroking the shot too softly carries its own perils. You may not separate the cluster at all, or cause the cue ball to freeze against one of the object balls, or end up with the cue ball too close to another ball for there to be a viable shot.

How can you develop a sense of how hard you will need to stroke the cue ball in order to separate a cluster at the right speed? Two factors must be considered: how thick or thin your hit on the object ball will be, and whether or not the balls in the cluster are frozen to one another (since frozen clusters require less force to separate).

• Adjusting the Speed of the Cue Ball •

The first step is to figure out what the tangent line between the cue ball and object ball will be at the moment of contact. In illustration 61, the tangent line between the cue ball and object ball at contact naturally moves the cue ball directly into the cluster you are trying to separate. All that is necessary is a center-ball hit. In illustration 62, however, you will need the cue ball to move forward of the tangent line, so you must apply follow. In illustration 63, a center-ball hit again will not do. You'll need for the cue ball to travel behind the natural path of the cue ball. To accomplish this movement behind the tangent line, you must apply draw.

Let's look at illustration 64. The tangent line between the cue ball and the object ball is heading directly towards the cluster, but the cue ball will be making a very full hit on object ball A. On a full hit such as this, much of the energy imparted to the cue ball will be

Illustration 61

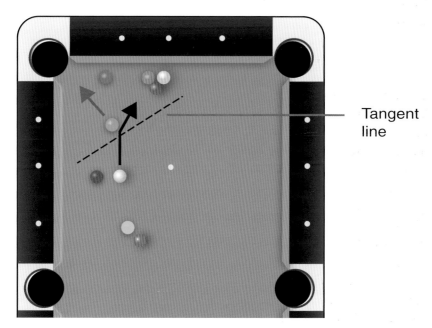

Tangent
line

Illustration 62

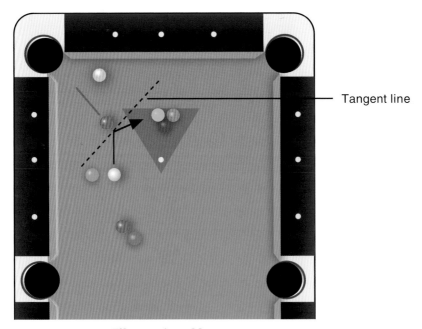

Tangent line

Illustration 63

absorbed by the object ball. For this reason, in order to get the cue ball to travel to the cluster with sufficient speed to separate the cluster, you will need to stroke this shot with authority.

Illustration 65 presents a different situation. Here, your shot involves a thin cut. On thin hits such as this, very little of the cue ball's energy is absorbed by the shot, leaving plenty of force to attack the cluster. On these types of thin hits, a softer stroke will do; anything more than that will lower your chances of being in position for your next shot.

• When to Separate Clusters of Balls •

You should always try to solve any problem areas in a rack, such as a cluster, at the earliest possible opportunity. Whether you are playing nine-ball, straight pool, or eight-ball, as soon as the rack is broken, look to see whether there are any problem clusters on the table. If so, you will need to get to work on them right away.

Take a look at illustration 66. Let's assume you're playing straight pool, in which you can pocket any ball you wish. Given your layout, you stand no chance of running out the table unless you take care of the problem created by the clot of balls at the end of

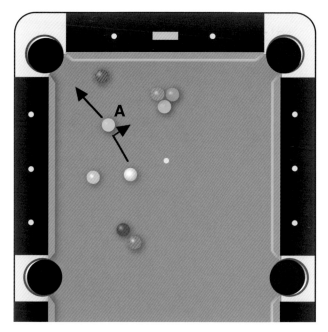

Illustration 64

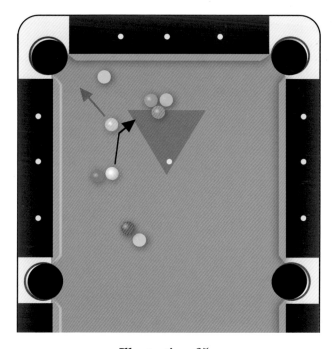

Illustration 65

the table. Even though you have a choice of shots and will likely
have more than one opportunity to separate the cluster, why squan-
der the chance you have now? From the position you're in, you can
separate the cluster by playing ball A into the right corner pocket.
You won't need to rely on whether you're able to get proper position on another shot in order to take apart the cluster. Attack it
now. Shoot ball A first.

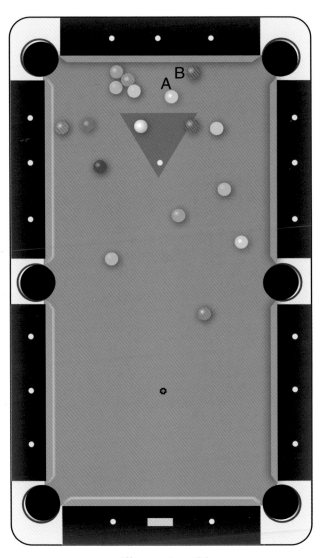

Illustration 66

Another advantage to shooting ball A in illustration 66 is the fact that ball B is in ideal position to serve as an "insurance" or "safety valve" shot. When the cue ball runs into the cluster after pocketing ball A, you may—or may not—end up with a shot on any of the balls that had formed the cluster. There is no guarantee that you'll have a shot on one of those balls. As long as you do not stroke the shot too hard, however, you *are* guaranteed a shot on ball B. That is why shots of this type are called insurance shots or safety valves. They provide absolute certainty that you will be able to shoot again after you make the shot at hand.

• When to "Bump" (Run the Cue Ball Into) Other Balls •

Let's say that you are in a situation where you need the cue ball to stay in the same general vicinity as your initial shot. The angle on each of the shots available to you, however, all involve thin cuts. In other words, none of your available shots involves a full hit. This means that you cannot merely stop the cue ball using the center-ball hit described in Chapter 5. Illustration 67 shows just such a situation. Let's say that you've decided your next shot will be ball X, because you can make the shot on an easy combination if you stay in the same neighborhood. If the cue ball rolls to the other side of the side pockets, however, you will have no shot on ball X.

While you have the luxury of a choice of several shots in illustration 67, how do we make sure the cue ball hangs around for a shot on ball X? If you shoot ball B, you'll be too far up the table for a shot on the combination on ball X. Similarly, if you shoot ball C, the cue ball will cut ball C thinly and then bounce off the rail and again, head up table. The answer is to take ball A first. Although shooting ball A also involves a thin cut, the tangent line on the shot runs the cue ball directly into ball D. By using ball D to stop the cue ball, you will end up in ideal shape for the combination on ball X. As a bonus, you will break up balls D and E, which cannot be made as they presently lie.

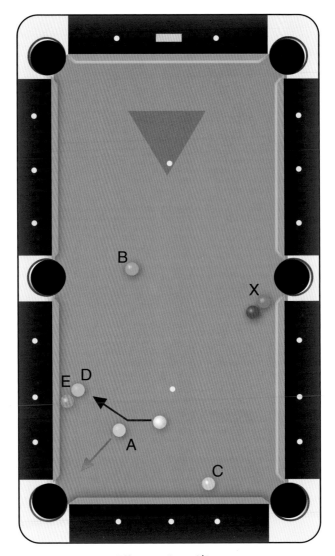

Illustration 67

• Choosing *Not* to Run
Into Object Balls •

It takes foresight and discipline to plan to separate problem clusters in a frame at the earliest possible opportunity. Every successful player attacks these types of problems right away. Even among skilled players, however, many lack the discipline to leave well enough alone in some situations.

The rule to remember is that if a ball can be pocketed as it lies, do not disturb it. In illustration 68, you're playing eight-ball and need to pocket the striped balls first. Some players will see the five balls grouped near the lower right-hand corner pocket as a threat and blast into those balls, while shooting ball A into the side pocket. By studying the five grouped balls for a moment, however, you will see that ball C can be pocketed in corner pocket X even though ball

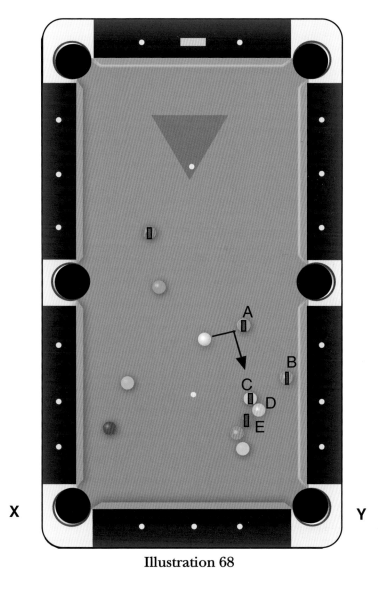

Illustration 68

C is frozen to ball D. It is true that running the cue ball into the five balls may result in an easier layout. What the better players understand is that doing so may also create a more difficult layout. The better plan is to get to ball C as soon as possible. In this instance, you're fortunate enough to have ball B available to help you do so. Simply pocket ball A with a bit of follow, shoot ball B next, again following slightly, and then pick off ball C. Once you make C, you can make ball E into pocket Y. The same type of pattern could be used if you were playing straight pool.

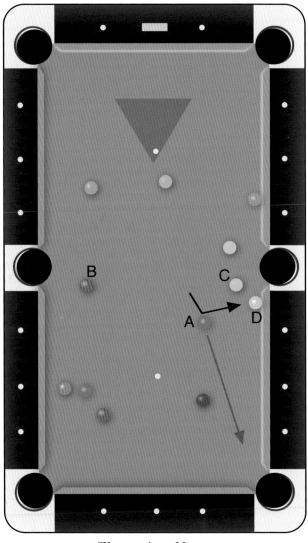

Illustration 69

Illustration 69 depicts another situation where you'll be better off thinking a little before disrupting the layout. This time you're playing straight pool. In the illustration, ball D lies in a terrible spot. Since it is so near the side pocket, ball D cannot be pocketed easily in any of the six pockets. When confronted with this layout, you should be concerned about how to move or pocket ball D as soon as possible. The quickest way would be to attack ball D on the very first shot. One way to do so would be by pocketing ball A in the corner and running into D, as shown in the illustration. This is a

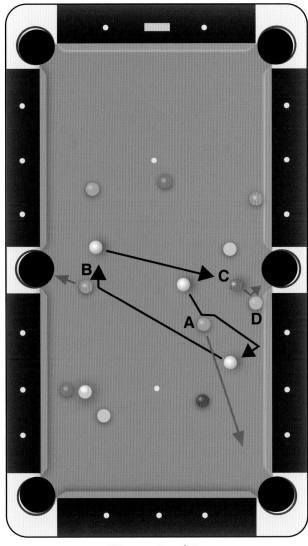

Illustration 70

poor choice, however, since you may create a new problem—causing ball D to tie up ball C—as you're solving another.

You could also attack ball D by playing ball C *off* of ball D, an easy shot to make, which will also bump D off of its spot on the rail. The problem with taking this shot as your first one in this frame is that ball D may tie up ball A when it comes off the rail. Here, you may be best served by a little patience. Illustration 70 shows the pattern. Start by shooting ball A in the corner pocket, then pocket ball B in the left side pocket. Now, you're in ideal position to play ball C off ball D. This time, however, the table is a little less cluttered. If you move ball D with the right speed (softly), it cannot tie up any other shot on the table. At the same time, you have not waited too long into the pattern to move D, since you have lots of next-shot opportunities available after you make C in the side.

• The Essentials •

1. Immediately after the balls are broken, study whether there are any problems in the layout, such as clusters. Do this whether or not you are the player at the table.

2. When planning to separate a cluster, choose a pattern that allows you the security of an insurance ball.

3. Gauge how much speed you will need when separating clusters based on how full or how thinly your cue ball will be contacting the object ball.

4. Stay disciplined enough to pass up trying to move object balls when those balls can be pocketed as they lie.

9

The Other 80 Percent— Thinking Your Way Through a Pool Game

The mental aspect of pool can be broken up into two parts: analyzing racks and achieving the proper state of mind. Analyzing racks and the patterns within racks is the mental nuts and bolts of playing pool. It involves examining the layouts of tables and figuring out the best way to clear them. Achieving the proper state of mind is more metaphysical. The proper state of mind is always accurately described in contradictory terms. The goal is to achieve a state of relaxed concentration. You want to be tense enough to be aware of, and concerned about, what is going on . . . yet calm enough to allow yourself to execute your shots with fluidity and touch.

Specific strategies for how to think through running racks of straight pool, eight-ball, and nine-ball are addressed in the next chapter. Here, we'll focus on more general concepts concerning the mental aspect of the game—things to keep in mind when playing any of the various games.

• Relaxed Concentration •

On any given day, a player is likely to miss shots because he or she is too tense or—on that same day—miss shots due to carelessness, or being too relaxed. Striking the right balance is not always easy to do, but there are strategies you can adopt to give yourself the best chance to achieve that balance most of the time.

When playing, focus on your routine for aiming, setting up for shots, and taking practice strokes. Focusing on this physical routine will be reassuring and nearly hypnotic even when you might be prone to nervousness, such as when you are aware people are watching you play or you're competing in a tournament. Also, simply thinking about the most elemental mechanical parts of your game will help you to concentrate on the task at hand rather than any distractions. You will need to learn how to play well even when you are aware of an audience, but it will be impossible to play well if you are dwelling on the fact that you are being watched.

Reaching a state of relaxed concentration also requires that you gain a sense of touch when you are playing. This sense of touch grows out of forcing yourself to be aware of every aspect of what is going on on the table: how fast the table is playing, how the weight of the cue feels in your back hand, how the tip of the cue feels at impact, how the object balls react to the cue ball, how easily the object balls are separating, how the cue ball and object balls react off the cushions, and the like.

Besides being aware of what is happening after you stroke the cue ball, you must anticipate and visualize—before you stroke the cue ball—what is going to happen when you do stroke the shot. Think about what your goals are for the shot. For example, you may want to follow the cue ball five inches so that it lands near the head spot on a given shot. If so, *before* you release your stroke, visualize the perfect execution of that shot—how heavy the cue ball will feel when struck with the perfect speed, how the cue ball will sound when it makes contact with the object ball, how the cue ball will slow down at impact—and then float to your position target. These mental images will train your mind and body to gauge your speed and your stroke. What's more, they will put you in the calm yet focused state of mind you will need to achieve in order to play your best.

• Trust Yourself •

Unfortunately, many players get their egos tied up with the game. Simply because they have achieved some skill at pool, they feel that they deserve the awe of everyone in the poolroom. You should avoid this type of attitude, but you *will* need to develop a sort of quiet faith about your own abilities. No matter how well you play, you should have confidence in what you know you can do. You must trust yourself. To do anything else will be an endless source of frustration, since players who think that they cannot make a shot usually find a way to prove themselves right.

Again, start by focusing on the mechanics. Go through your checklist for pinpointing the correct point of aim, getting into your shooting stance, and taking your practice strokes. Know that you have your feet, body, and head aligned perfectly for execution of the shot. If anything feels out of line, simply stand up . . . all the way up. Then start from the beginning.

By vowing to yourself that you will only shoot when you are ready, you will know that by the time you actually release your stroke, everything will be perfect. You will know exactly where you are aiming and how you will be delivering the cue ball to the desired spot.

Sometimes, in especially tense moments, you may find it hard to think clearly enough to be able to sort out where you're aiming, how you're standing, or whether you've taken your regular number of practice strokes. In these situations, make sure that your rear hand and arm are relaxed. This can be done by making sure that your rear hand is hanging directly below your elbow. Make sure you are not clutching the cue. If you cannot feel the weight of the cue, you are gripping it too tightly. Shake or jiggle your rear hand until you can feel the weight of the back end of the cue.

Having relaxed your body to this point, give yourself an aiming point on the object ball and a position goal for the cue ball. Play position even if you are shooting game ball and don't need to play position. The strangest things happen when a player is nervous, like scratching or miscuing. That's why you're always better off having a plan for where you want the cue ball to go. While you're taking your practice shots, check again to be sure that you can feel the weight of the cue in your rear hand. If so, let the stroke go.

• The Essentials •

1. Learn to relax through focusing on your routines for aiming, setting up for shots, and taking practice strokes.

2. Develop your sense of touch by visualizing before each shot, and becoming aware of every aspect of what is going on on the table.

3. Shoot only when you are confident that you have de- termined the proper aiming point and your body is perfectly aligned to take the shot. Once you are sure that you are prepared to shoot, trust your own ability to execute.

Straight Pool, Eight-Ball, and Nine-Ball— The Rules of the Game and Beyond

There are literally dozens of games and variations of games that are played on a pool table. I'm going to focus here on straight pool, nine-ball, and eight-ball because they are three of the most popular games, and because they are games that can be enjoyed at all levels of ability. One-pocket is an example of a game that is close to straight pool in popularity, but a difficult game to tackle without a significant level of expertise in one of the other games.

Should your interest in billiards grow, you may also become enchanted with the beautiful and intriguing billiard games that are played on a carom table; that is, a billiard table without pockets. I played both pool (pocket billiards) and three-cushion billiards (the most popular carom game in the United States). Since this book's focus is on pool, however, we will stick to pocket billiards games.

Chapter 1 lists some general rules and terminology applicable to all pool games. If you are completely unfamiliar with pool, you may want to read that chapter again before continuing, as we take a tour of three major pool games: straight pool, nine-ball, and eight-ball.

• Straight Pool •

Straight pool is the purist's game. According to the Billiards Congress of America, it "is generally considered to be the game that provides the greatest all-around test of complete pocket-billiards playing skill, requiring great concentration, accuracy, shot-making, defense, patience, and knowledge." As such, it is a terrific game to learn from. Unlike eight-ball and nine-ball, which are one-rack games, in straight pool the competitors play through rack after rack to try to reach a designated point total (such as 75, 100, or 150 points). You can shoot at any ball on the table but must "call" each shot by designating the ball you intend to pocket, as well as the intended pocket. Whether you will be playing a combination, carom, or bank does not need to be called—only the ball and the pocket. Each legally pocketed ball scores one point. Many of the principles basic to straight pool, such as separating problem clusters, should be kept in mind for eight-ball and nine-ball as well.

Straight pool, also called "14.1 Continuous" or "14.1," uses all fifteen object balls. After all but one of the object balls have been pocketed, the last object ball of the rack (the "break ball") and the cue ball are left where they lie, and the remaining fourteen balls are re-racked. Then, the break shot follows. Here your intention is to try to pocket the break ball and, in the same shot, drive the cue ball into the rack to separate out additional object balls for more shots so your inning can continue.

The Opening Break in Straight Pool

On the opening break, the object balls are racked with the first ball of the triangle on the foot spot. The cue ball may be placed anywhere behind the head string (the portion of the table shaded in illustration 71). Making a called shot on the opening break is

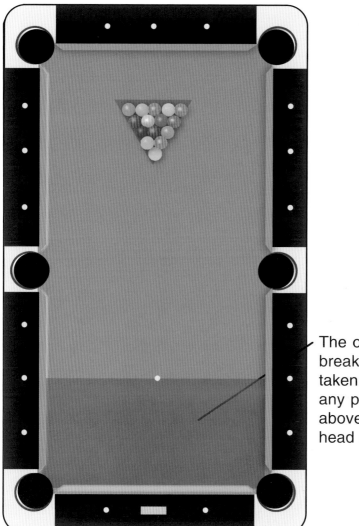

The opening break may be taken from any place above the head string.

Illustration 71

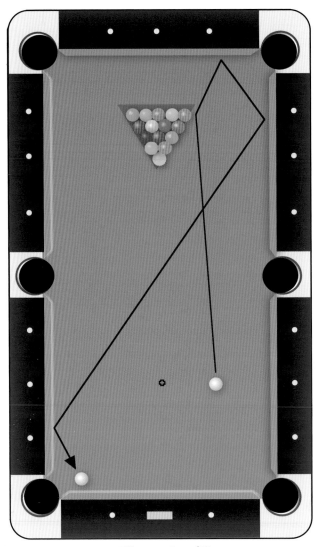

Illustration 72

unlikely, so the standard opening is a safe. The goal is to graze one of the corners of the rack with running english, sending the cue ball three rails and up to the head rail as shown in illustration 72. Although the illustration shows the safety played off the right corner ball with right english, the shot may be played just as effectively off of the left corner ball with left english (running english).

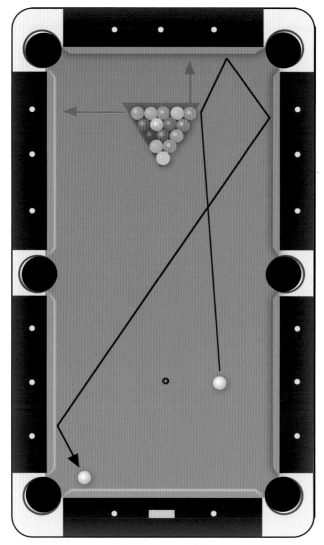

Illustration 73

On this opening break, at least two object balls must hit a rail, in addition to the cue ball. Ideally, very little of the rack is disturbed except for the two corner balls. If struck perfectly, the corner balls move straight out to the rails and then obediently return to nearly their original locations in the rack, as shown in illustration 73. You will want to hit about one-quarter of the corner ball with the cue ball. Hitting the corner ball too full will loosen too many object balls for potential shots for your opponent, and hitting the corner too thin will risk that the object balls do not reach a rail.

On the opening break, as with most safety shots in a pool game, if you concentrate on where the cue ball ends up you will fare well. Try to get the cue ball frozen or nearly frozen to the head rail. If you succeed at leaving the cue ball there, your opponent will be left with a tough shot even if a ball or two loosens inadvertently from the rack.

Straight Pool Offense

After the opening break, break shots are created by leaving the last object ball in each frame and the cue ball in position so that, after the remaining fourteen balls are re-racked, you can sink the break shot and open up the rack to pocket balls from the new frame. If you are truly a charmed individual, you will be able to leave yourself the ideal break shot shown in illustration 74 most of the time. This is unlikely, but there are plenty of other possibilities, such as those shown in illustrations 75, 76, 77, 78, and 79.

The key on your break shots is to try to send the cue ball into one of the three corners of the rack so it is easier to separate object balls for shots without the cue ball getting stuck against the rack. Most break shots can be made successfully with a medium speed. Don't make the novice's mistake of slamming the cue ball into the rack on all of your break shots. If the cue ball meets the rack at one of its corners, a moderate but *smooth* stroke will free up shots without sending the cue ball around the table pinball-style. Controlling your break shots in this way will minimize your risk of scratching or leaving yourself with long shots. As with any other shot, stroking a break shot with too much speed makes it less likely that you will pocket the object ball. You will generally need to stroke your break shots more firmly than your other shots, but strive to use the minimum speed that will get the job done.

Once the rack is open, you must immediately go to work! Most players do not go to work soon enough. By that I mean that as soon as the rack is broken, you must study the layout for problems, and then immediately start working on solving them. Problems include object balls clustered together, balls that block other balls from a

An ideal break shot.

Illustration 74

Another good break shot opportunity. This time, you shoot the object ball into the side pocket.

Illustration 75

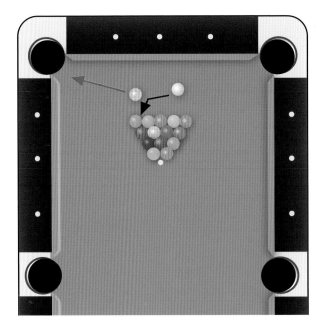

A behind-the-rack break shot. One of the easiest break shots to pocket.

Illustration 76

The mirror image of the break shot shown in illustration 74. This shot is just as ideal, and even better than the shot in illustration 74 for a left-handed player, since it's an easier reach for left-handers.

Illustration 77

This break shot uses the rail. By driving the cue ball into the corner of the rack, you improve your chances of freeing the cue ball for shot opportunities after the break. A touch of draw and left english will bring the cue ball back to the desired part of the rack.

Illustration 78

Stroke the cue ball firmly just below center to bring it off the top corner of the rack.

Illustration 79

pocket, and balls sitting near the rail. Balls on the rail are problems because they can be easily pocketed in (at most) two pockets. Often, they can be made easily into only one of the pockets. Balls on the rail are also a nuisance because other object balls tend to become clustered with them during the course of a rack.

If there are balls knotted together in clusters, you must look for object balls nearby that you can use as mini-break balls—shots off of which you can separate the clusters. Look at illustration 80.

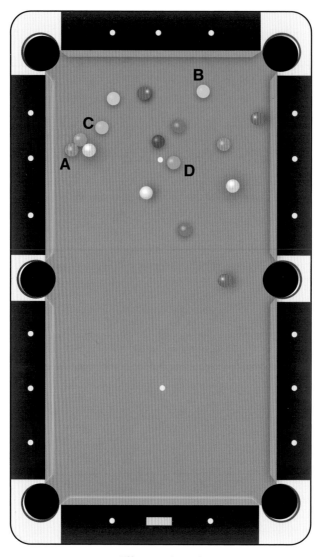

Illustration 80

Here, you are very fortunate because there is only one cluster in the layout—ball A and the two other balls stuck near it. Ball C is nearby and could be used to break up the cluster, so your first goal in this layout should be to get a shot on ball C with the proper angle to separate the cluster. You have a great chance to do that right away by playing ball D in the corner and stopping the cue ball. After D, you'll be in perfect shape to cut ball C into the corner and separate

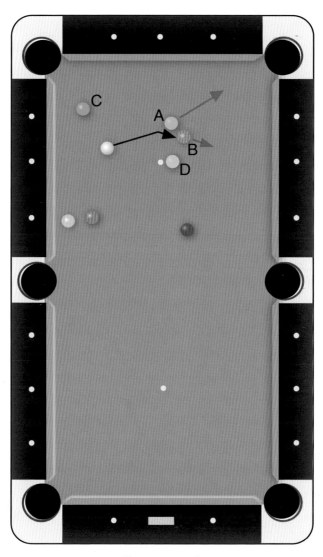

Illustration 81

the cluster. This pattern works well because you're bound to have a shot on ball B after shooting the mini-break shot (ball C).

Going to work right away also means creating break balls if the layout does not present one. To do this, you must consider whether there are balls that can be nudged into position so that they become break balls. Illustration 81 shows an example. The layout you're left with here has no problem clusters, but balls A, B, and D are not available as break balls since they're within the rack area. The angle you have on ball A, however, is perfect for allowing you to push ball B out for an ideal break ball while pocketing ball A in the corner. You are also guaranteed a shot on either ball C or ball D after you sink A.

If possible, try to get a little work done with each shot. With each available shot, start working your way towards your mini-break balls. Don't waste opportunities by just mindlessly making the easiest possible shots. If you do that, you'll find yourself near the end of the rack with problems left on the table but no way to fix them.

Besides seeking to break up clusters and creating break balls, going to work early means that you should always try to clear out object balls that block other object balls from getting to a pocket. In illustration 82, you have lots of easy shots available and no balls clustered together. Ball C is your easiest shot of all, but you should not take it. Although you have no big problems, like clusters, you do have two object balls, balls A and B, that are blocking the pocket from other balls. Go to work right away by getting ball A out of the way while you're in position to do so. With draw, and perhaps some left english, you can pocket A and move the cue ball into a position from which you'll have several available shots, as shown in illustration 83.

Once all your problems in a frame have been cleared away, you're ready to start getting to your break ball. In illustration 84, no problems are left and you've got an excellent break ball in ball A. Ball B will be your "key" ball, the shot just before your break ball (the key ball is the last shot of the frame before the balls are re-racked). The goal, then, is to pick out the pattern that leads us to ball B most naturally. The easiest way to figure this out is to think backwards from B. The ball best-positioned to give us shape on ball B is ball F. Getting to ball F is easy from ball E. We can play position for E in the side off ball

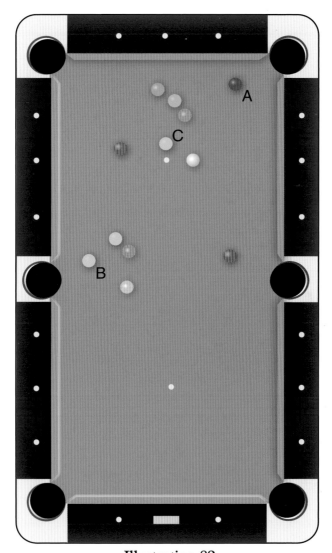

Illustration 82

D. Slight follow on ball C will give us position on ball D with the angle we want for playing ball E in the side.

   To summarize, play ball C first, shooting it into the corner with slight follow. After pocketing C, the layout will look like illustration 85. This position will allow you to pocket D in the corner with a stop stroke. Given the slight angle on ball D, the cue ball will move slightly to the right for a straight-in shot on ball E. From here, it's

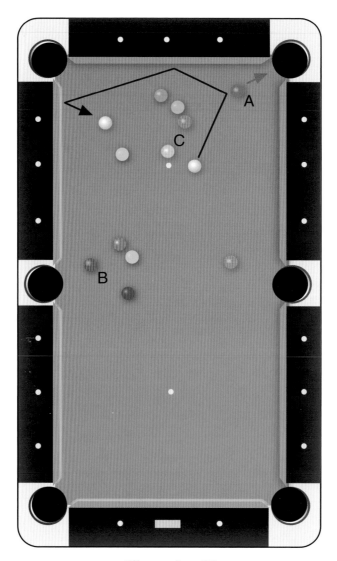

Illustration 83

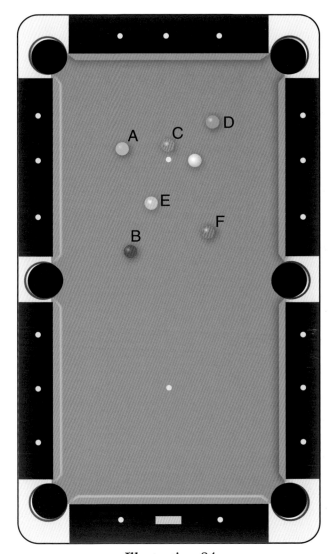

Illustration 84

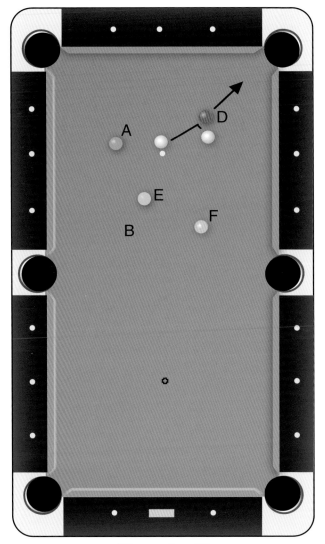

Illustration 85

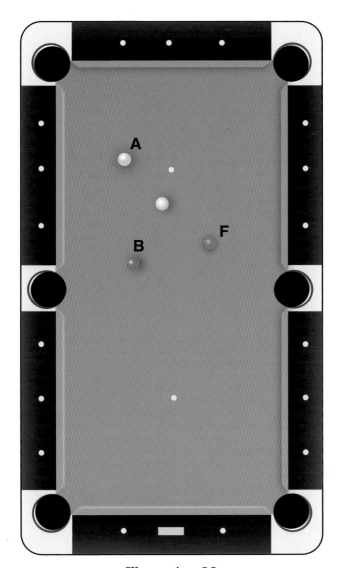

Illustration 86

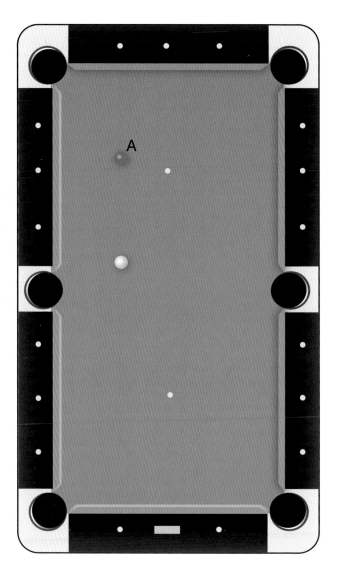

Illustration 87

stop-stop to ball B. In illustration 86, you've stopped the cue ball while pocketing E. Now, you're left with another stop shot on ball F for perfect position on B. You'll need to follow off ball B ever so slightly to get a favorable angle on your break ball, ball A. A center to low hit on the cue ball while shooting ball B will give you the desired follow (not too much) since the distance between the cue ball and B will allow the cue ball to pick up some forward rotation (as we discussed in chapter 5). The final result is shown in illustration 87.

Strategy

Although pool players can be either offensive or defensive in style, reduced to its simplest terms, there is only one strategy in straight pool: Try never to miss a called shot. An offensive-minded player does this mainly by confidently pocketing balls, and successfully falling onto break shots to move from rack to rack. A defensive-minded player aims to avoid missing a called shot mainly by carefully constructing runs, but playing safe if he or she is not 100 percent confident of pocketing a ball. "Mainly" is the crucial word here, because straight pool requires versatility. Someone who can merely pocket balls and cannot play effective safeties will lose just as quickly as someone who can play excellent safeties but cannot pocket balls. In the course of a game, even an offensive-minded player will be forced to play safeties along the way, just as defensive players must score 100 points, one way or another, to win a 100-point game.

Safeties

After the opening safety, a legal safety is executed when the cue ball or an object ball touches a cushion (or an object ball is pocketed) after the cue ball contacts any object ball. Although the requirements for a safety are not rigorous, playing a safety in straight pool requires care, since any ball on the table represents a potential shot for your opponent.

Your allies in playing a straight pool safety are distance and proximity. In illustration 88, my opponent has left me without a shot and near the lower left-hand corner of the table. One good response is to graze the edge of the rack and send the cue ball up to the head of the table. This is done by touching as little of the end ball as possible. Even if ball X moves away from the rack slightly, the distance between the cue ball and ball X will make any shot on ball X an unattractive one. Take a look at illustration 89. If my opponent

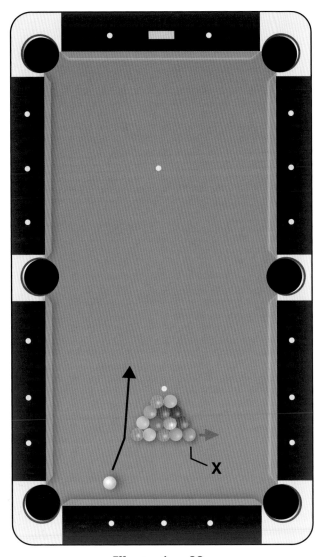

Illustration 88

does not understand the percentages, he will play the shot and either miss and leave me a better shot, or pocket ball X without disturbing the rack enough to continue his run.

To take this situation further, let's say that *you* are the incoming player faced with the layout in illustration 89. If shooting ball X is not the correct move, what is?

Illustration 89

Some players smart enough to pass up trying to break up the rack off a shot on ball X will play ball X nonetheless. They'll stroke the shot softly, realizing the rack won't open up but planning to play a safety on the next shot. This, too, is a losing strategy. Ball X is a tough shot no matter how you cut it, and you're more likely to miss and leave a shot on ball X than make it. Playing a

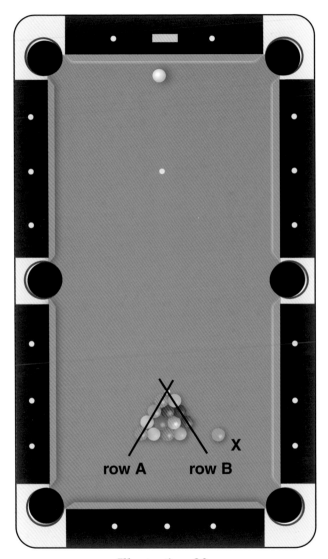

Illustration 90

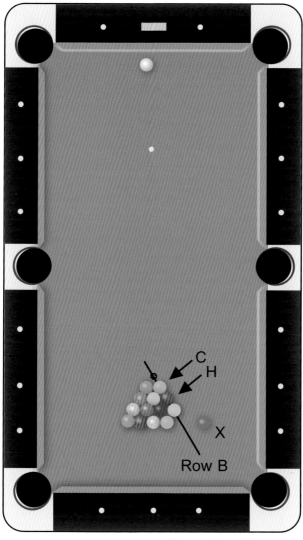

If the balls in row B are frozen, play safe against the row by rolling the cue ball into ball C as if you're trying to cut that ball into ball H.

Illustration 91

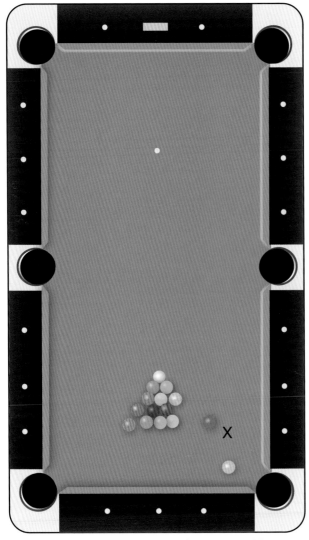

The safety resulting from rolling the cue ball against row B is shown.

Illustration 92

safety now is much easier than playing a tough shot on ball X and then trying a safe.

At least two safety options should be considered. Check to see if the balls along either of the outer rows of the rack are still frozen or near frozen (rows A or B in illustration 90). If one of them is, you can roll the cue ball against the upper-most ball in the row, as if you're trying to nudge that uppermost ball into the ball next to it in the outer row as shown in illustration 91.The cue ball should

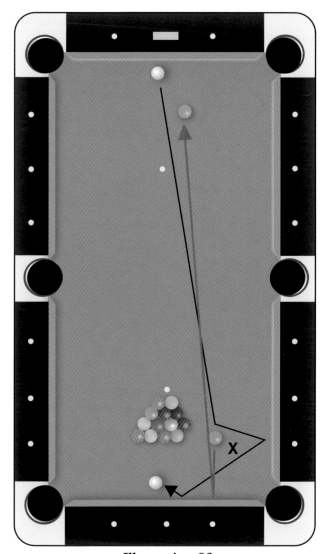

Illustration 93

stick right up against the rack, loosening the lowest ball in the rack, and perhaps one or two others, with that lowest ball ending up near the corner pocket. In the result depicted in illustration 92, ball X is still positioned on the other side of the rack, and all of the loose balls will make your opponent's attempt at a return safety much more difficult. Here, proximity allows the safety; with the cue frozen up against the upper corner of the rack, as shown in illustration 92, shots at the loose balls are blocked.

Option two is to bank ball X off of the foot rail so that X rolls up towards the head of the table, and, most importantly, the cue ball rolls to the side rail and comes to rest behind the rack. As we see in illustration 93, controlling the cue ball is the most important aspect of this safety. If the cue ball stops near the bottom rail and behind the rack, your opponent will be left without a shot even if ball X ends up near one of the upper corner pockets.

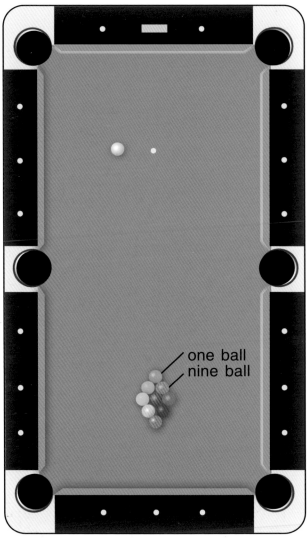

one ball
nine ball

Illustration 94

• Nine-Ball •

Nine-ball is the dominant tournament game today. The game utilizes only the balls numbered one through nine, which are racked in a diamond with the one ball on the foot spot and the nine ball in the center of the rack (illustration 94). Nine-ball is fast-paced, and forces players to attempt long shots, bank shots, combination shots, and generally tougher shots all around than the other pool games. Shots are not called, and any legally pocketed shot, on the break or otherwise, allows the shooter to continue.

For a legal shot, the shooter must contact the lowest ball on the table first and then either pocket a ball or drive an object ball or the cue ball to a cushion. Failing to do so, or scratching in a pocket, results in a foul; and three fouls in a row result in a loss of game. The object in nine-ball is to pocket the nine ball. Making any of the other balls counts for nothing. Your opponent may have sunk the one through the eight, but if he leaves you with an easy shot on the nine and you make it, you're the legitimate winner of the game.

The numbered balls, including the nine ball, need not be sunk in any particular order. If the lowest numbered ball is contacted first, and the nine ball is pocketed on the shot, the game is over. Thus, making the nine on the break wins the game since the nine is pocketed after the lowest ball on the table (the one) has been contacted first. Thus the game can be won if someone is lucky enough to have the nine ball fall on the break. Breaking effectively in nine-ball (in terms of spreading the object balls and controlling the cue ball) is a skill. Making the nine ball on the break is not. Many times when the nine ball falls on the break it is pure luck, such as when another moving object ball happens to knock it in.

• Strategy •

Although nine-ball experts include defensive specialists, nine-ball naturally lends itself to players who love to pocket balls from anywhere on the table. Usually, the penalty for a miss in nine-ball is not nearly as severe as it is in straight pool. In straight pool, a miss almost inevitably leads to a shot for the incoming player. In nine-ball, you may miss and leave the incoming player without an opportunity to touch the lowest-numbered ball, never mind pocket it.

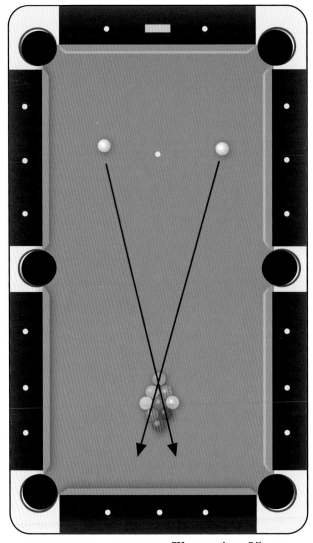

Hit the one ball full. This means shoot at the one as if you're aiming the cue ball straight through it.

Illustration 95

Other than keeping your eyes open for an opportunity to sink the nine ball off a combination or billiard, nine-ball offense boils down to breaking the balls effectively, and then finding a way to run the balls in sequence. To break, place the cue ball at a point along the head string. You will find that you are more likely to pocket balls on the break when you do not start with the cue ball on or near the head spot. No matter where you place the cue ball, aim for a full hit

Don't aim to hit the one ball straight back into the rack, as shown here. Where you should contact the one ball is going to depend on where you place the cue ball before you break.

Illustration 96

on the one ball. Illustration 95 shows two examples of a nice full hit on the one ball. Illustration 96 shows a common mistake.

Getting a shot off your break requires power, accuracy, cue ball control, and luck. You can only control the first three elements of an effective break, so let's focus on those. The first two, power and accuracy, cannot be separated. If you apply tons of speed to the cue ball but fail to hit the one squarely, a lot of the power of the cue ball will be lost. Transferring power from the speed of the cue ball into an impact upon the rack requires accuracy—a perfectly full hit. If the cue ball lacks speed, even a full hit results in a weak break.

Power is achieved through proper mechanics. Just as the break stands alone from every other pool stroke, so should the mechanics of a break also be unique. To break the balls hard you'll need to allow your rear hand to come through the stroke as freely as possible. That means you must stand up straighter in your stance and move your rear hand further back on your cue stick than for all other types of shots. You cannot rely only on your arm muscles for a solid break. Your legs and body weight must contribute, too. This is done by starting with the weight of your body mainly on the rear leg. During the stroke, shift your weight to your front leg. Timing is critical, so, as always, establish a routine and a rhythm for the stroke. Take the same number of practice strokes on your break every time. As with every other stroke, don't dwell on the break shot. Establish your routine and stick to it.

Accuracy on the break requires a solid bridge. If the cue stick wavers on the break, accuracy naturally goes out the window. Check your bridge by taking your rear hand off the back of the cue stick, allowing the stick to rest on the table. Next, wriggle the shaft of the stick from side to side while it is still in your bridge. You should not be able to move the stick very much.

Accuracy also requires self-control. Don't unleash every ounce of cue ball speed at your disposal. Only use that amount of power you can consistently focus on the pinhead-sized target on the nose of the one ball.

Cue ball control is an important ingredient of a good nine-ball break. If the cue ball flies around the table on your break, you will often scratch or end up without a shot on the one ball. The best you can achieve is for the cue ball to stroke the one fully, and then back up slightly so it ends up in the center of the table. From there, any shot on the lowest ball left on the table will be relatively short.

Where you contact the cue ball in order to get this effect is different for each player. To find out the right spot for you, practice by breaking the balls several times using a center-ball hit. If the cue ball lurches ahead after contact, aim at a lower point on the cue ball on the next try. If the cue ball retreats to the head of the table after hitting the rack, make the opposite adjustment and aim higher on the cue ball.

After the break, begin by looking for problems. Is there a cluster of balls stuck together? Is there an object ball that is difficult to get to because of the way other balls are situated? Then consider possible solutions. Perhaps the balls in a cluster can be picked off if you can get position on a particular side of the cluster. Perhaps there are shots available near the cluster that will allow you to separate the cluster in the course of your run. Perhaps you will be able to avoid problem areas in the rack altogether by pocketing the nine on a combination or carom.

If the layout does not offer an opportunity to solve problems along the way, figure out where in your sequence you should play safe. The same clusters that aggravate you when you're trying to run the balls become helpful when you turn to trying to play a safety.

Other than making provisions for solving problems along the way, running a rack of nine-ball does not require tremendous foresight. For many players, it simplifies the game to think about only three things at a time: the ball you're shooting, your next shot, and the angle you want on that second shot so that you can get position on your third shot.

In the layout shown in illustration 97, you're shooting at the five ball. The three balls to keep in mind are the five, six, and seven. Making the five and getting a shot on the six is not a problem, but the third and crucial consideration is to figure out what angle you want on the six to achieve position on the seven. The answer is that you want the cue ball to fall on the left side of the gray line running between the six ball and the pocket. By maintaining such an angle, you can draw off the side rail for natural position on the seven.

Now look at illustration 98, which is your layout after you've pocketed the five ball. The three shots to keep in mind now are the six, seven, and eight. You will be playing the six in the corner pocket and the seven in the lower left corner pocket, but must now think about what angle you want on the seven to get position on the eight. Here, *no* angle is best. If you can end up straight on the seven ball, you will be able to land in place for a shot on the eight without leaving the cue ball on the rail closest to the seven ball. Stroke the cue ball at the six with slight draw and you will align yourself perfectly for the seven.

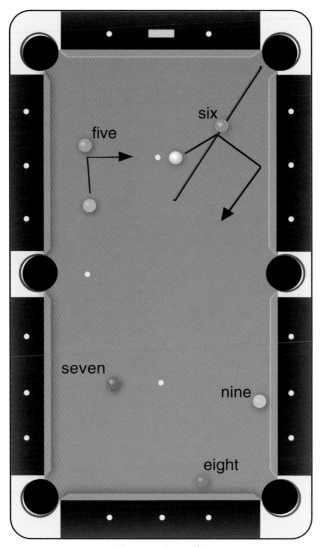

Illustration 97

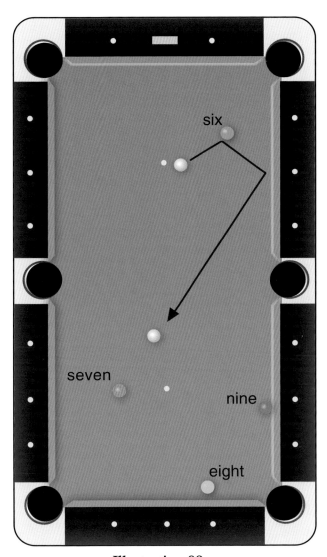

Illustration 98

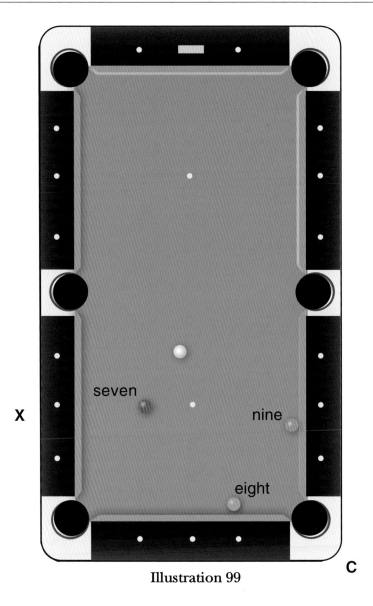

Illustration 99

So far, we've only pocketed two balls, the five and the six, but we've planned out shots based on the position of four of the balls: the five, six, seven, and eight. Since we're down to the final three balls of the frame, we're finally ready to finish off the rack.

In illustration 99, you've made the six and you're ready to sink the seven in the corner. First you must consider, however, what angle you want on the eight ball to achieve position on the nine ball. Although this looks simple, the remaining three balls deserve some thought.

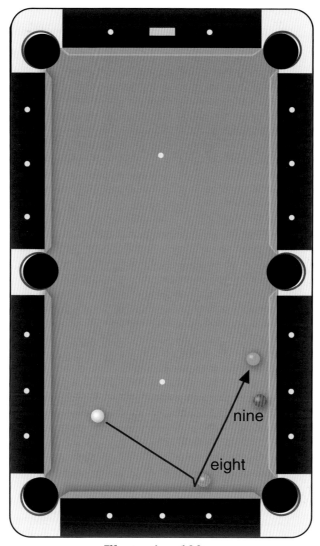

Illustration 100

You cannot merely stop the cue ball off the seven since your shot on the eight will be too angled. That would make the eight tougher to pocket than it needs to be, and will also require the cue ball to travel all the way up to the head of the table and then back down for position on the nine. On the other hand, if you follow the cue ball too much off the seven, you will end up too straight on the eight, making it difficult or impossible to move the cue ball above the nine for a shot in pocket C.

To find the exact angle you want off the eight ball, walk over to point X *before* you start lining up your shot on the seven. From point X, make up your mind which angle on the eight would be ideal. Then, before you leave X, come up with a measurement or reference point of some kind. In this example, one way of doing this is to tell yourself silently that the cue ball will follow four inches forward after contacting the seven. Or, you can make your goal to roll the cue ball until it is halfway between the first and second diamonds on the side rail. Another reference would be to roll the cue ball until it is on the line connecting the eight ball and the second diamond on the side rail near X. However you choose to tell yourself what the position goal should be, give yourself a precise target.

Illustration 100 shows the results of your effort. The seven is off the table, and you are left with a natural angle on the eight ball to gently follow the cue ball one-rail to the nine. This completes your run-out from the five ball!

By thinking of a nine-ball frame just three balls at a time, you will be able to thread your way through an entire rack without becoming overwhelmed at the prospect of running all nine balls in sequence. As in any of the games, just make sure that you have scouted out any problems on the table before taking your first shot.

Nine-ball Safety Play and "Kicking"

Since three fouls in a row by the same player result in loss of game, nine-ball allows a player to win based purely on safety play. Nine-ball safety play seems fairly simple since you need to hide only one ball—the lowest-numbered one—from your opponent. Since the game involves only nine balls, however, there aren't too many balls to hide the cue ball behind!

With the three-foul rule in effect, you also have to learn how to make a hit on the lowest-numbered object ball when someone has played you safe. If your opponent has played a good safety, making a legal hit usually requires going rail-first with the cue ball. This is called "kicking." You'll find it necessary to play rail-first shots only occasionally in straight pool or eight-ball, but you must learn to kick well to play nine-ball. Kicking with the goal of merely touching the lowest-numbered ball on the table will suffice in a match between players of modest skill. As you progress at the game, however, you will need to accomplish specific goals through your kicks, such as playing a return safety, giving yourself the best possible chance to pocket the object ball, and the like. In a good nine-ball game, the contestants often engage in a war of safeties and kicks until one of the players finally has an opening to try to run balls off the table to get to the nine.

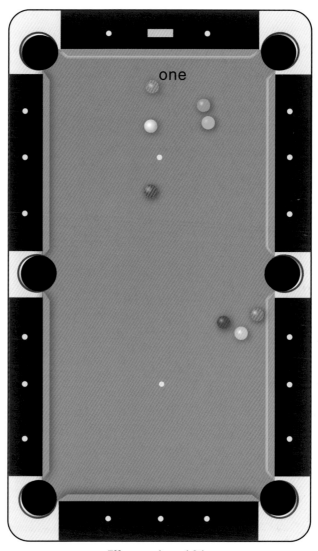

Illustration 101

Many of the principles discussed thus far apply to kicks. In order to accomplish certain kick shots you may need to widen the angle the cue ball takes off the rail. You can do this by stroking with running english or by taking speed off the cue ball. If you're playing safe off your kick, you may want the cue ball to stop in the area where it contacts the object ball. If that's the case, you'll need to make sure that the cue ball makes a full hit on the object ball. On

H

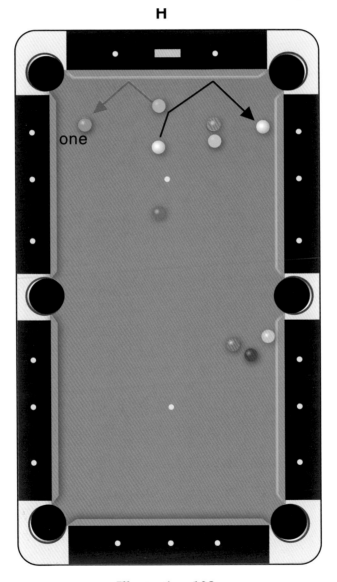

one

Illustration 102

the other hand, if you're playing a safety off a kick that requires the cue ball to roll across the table after contacting the object ball, a thin hit is a must.

In nine-ball safety play, as in straight pool, using distance is helpful. In illustration 101, two safety options off the one ball are available. The first is to play the cue ball off the right side of the one

H

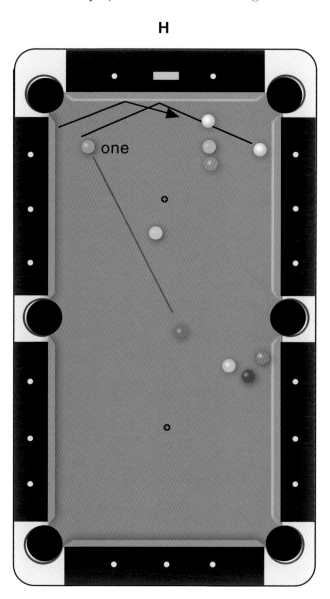

Illustration 103

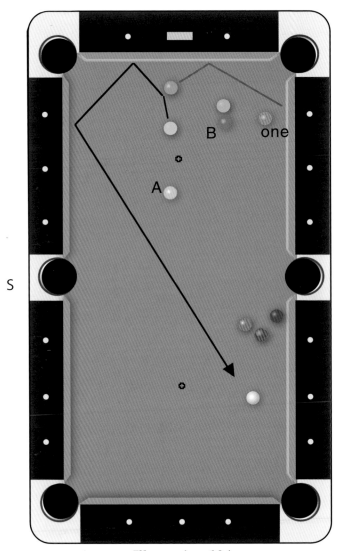

Illustration 104

in order to move the cue ball behind the two object balls to the right of the cue ball. In illustration 102, you've done just that. While you've hidden the one ball, the one and the cue ball remain relatively close together, and your opponent has a high-percentage kick shot available off rail H. Indeed, if your opponent wisely tries to kick into the right side of the one ball, she may leave you safe right back! (See illustration 103.)

From illustration 101, a safety that leaves your opponent further from the one ball is available by going off of the *left* side of the one ball. By doing so, you can run the cue ball (using left english) two rails to the other side of the table behind the three balls hanging around the side pocket. Illustration 104 shows the result of this superior safety. Even if you don't stroke this safety perfectly and your opponent is able to see part of the one ball, there is no guarantee that he or she will have a desirable shot. This is partly because you've left your opponent with more distance between the cue ball and the one. If the safety turns out as well as it is shown in the illustration, your opponent will have a very difficult time making any kind of contact on the one ball, since side pocket S makes it tough to kick off the left rail. Depending upon exactly where the one ball ends up, balls A and B may also become obstacles to your opponent's efforts to kick at the one. Also, the three balls in front of the cue ball make kicking off the right rail an impossibility.

Given nine-ball's three-scratch rule, sometimes the best offense is a good defense. Even if your preferred style of nine-ball is to run balls, you must also strengthen your safety game in order to win consistently.

• Eight-Ball •

Eight-ball is the one game that every pool player has tried at one time or another. The same cannot be said of any of the other billiard games. What eight-ball enjoys in terms of being widespread, however, it lacks in terms of consistency when it comes to the rules of the game.

While the Billiard Congress of America (BCA) provides a set of rules for eight-ball, the rules of this game vary widely from place to place. It is important to make sure that you and your opponent understand the "house" rules; that is, the rules governing the particular tournament, poolroom, or bar in which you are playing.

You should count on at least the following uniform rules: All fifteen balls are racked with the eight ball in the center and the striped balls and solid-colored balls distributed randomly around the eight, except that the lower corner balls should not both be solid or striped. The break is an open break, meaning that no shot must be called, and if any balls are pocketed on the break, the shooter continues. (The BCA rules dictate that the choice of stripes or solids is not determined by the break even if balls from one or both groups are pocketed on the break. Local house rules, however, often require the player who breaks to accept the group from which he or she has made the most balls.) If no balls are pocketed, the incoming player has a choice between the striped balls (called "highs" since they are numbered nine through fifteen) or the solid balls other than the eight ball (the "lows," numbered one through seven). Once a player has pocketed all of the balls in his or her group, but not sooner, the player must call and pocket the eight ball to win the game. If a player pockets the eight ball before pocketing all of the balls in his or her group, or pockets the eight in an unintended pocket, or makes the eight while pocketing his last object ball, that player loses the game.

Virtually everything beyond the above is left to whatever the house rules provide. This means you must clarify the following before starting an eight-ball game:

- what happens if someone makes the eight ball on the break;
- whether the breaker is free to choose either group if he or she makes more balls from one group on the break than the other;
- whether the shots before the eight ball must be called;
- whether players must announce, prior to the shot, if they will be playing a combination shot, billiard, or bank shot (a requirement not imposed by nine-ball or straight pool); and any number of other rules.

Strategy

For the purposes of understanding the most important strategies and safeties in this game, these local rules do not make much of a difference. One thing is clear: Although eight-ball is played by virtually everyone and was never the focus of tournament play, it is not an easy game. When is it most difficult? When your opponent has all or most of his or her balls still on the table. In that situation, you will be forced to navigate around your opponent's balls in your efforts to try to sink all of the balls in your own group, and finally, the eight ball. Tougher still is the case when you are the incoming player and have only a ball or two left, since you have very few patterns or sequences available to you to get to the eight ball.

This leads us to the overriding strategy of eight-ball: If you cannot see yourself winning the game from the layout you are facing,

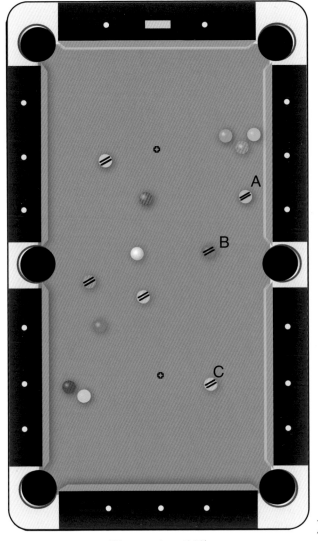

Illustration 105

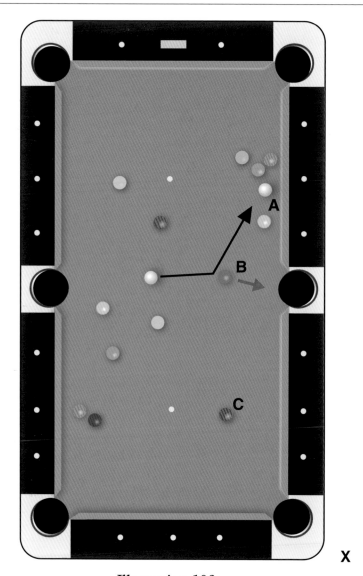

Illustration 106

do not pocket all (or most) of the balls in your group. If you cannot run out from your current position, make sure that you will have some chance of being left with a shot if you do get another chance. To do this, you must leave balls on the table. Following this simple rule gives you a better chance to win if you get another inning, and deprives your opponent of a clear playing field, making it more likely that he or she will be forced to hand the table back to you.

In illustration 105, there are six stripes and six solids remaining on the table. Let's first imagine that you are shooting at stripes. Examining the layout, you'll see that only one of the stripes is poorly positioned—ball A. The difficulty with ball A is that the two balls above it on the rail block ball A from the nearest corner pocket. Even though ball A is a problem, the cue ball is sitting in a spot from which you can get to ball A immediately. Since you have a slight angle on ball B in the side pocket, you can shoot B in the side

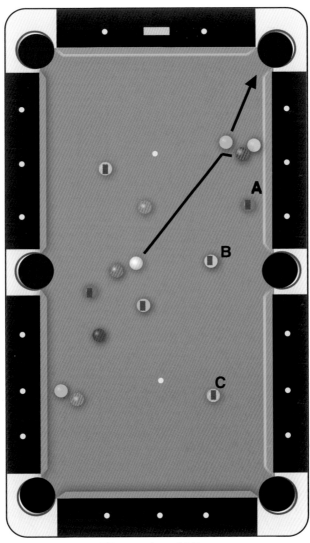

Illustration 107

and move the cue ball to just above A, for a shot at A down the long rail on the right into corner pocket X. Now let's look at illustration 106. Since you're able to get to your only problem ball right away, if handed the layout in illustration 105, you should try to run the stripes out from that position. Just be mindful of the fact that the eight ball (the solid black ball in the illustration) cannot be pocketed in the lower left corner because of the two solid balls sitting in the way. For that reason, you'll need to pay attention to how you get

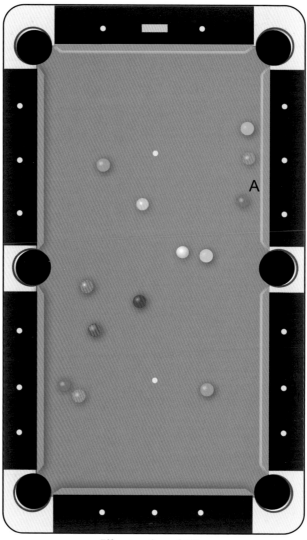

Illustration 108

position on the final eight ball shot in the frame. A good idea would be to leave ball C for your key ball so that you can play the eight in the side for the game-winning shot.

There is more to think about, however. When you're playing ball B in the side to get position on ball A, try to avoid separating the two solid balls clustered together at the upper right portion of the table. You don't want to solve problems for your opponent! By

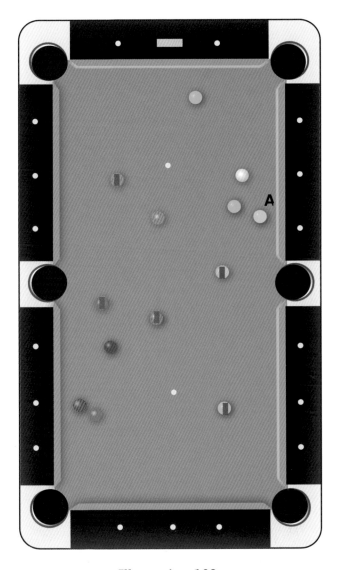

Illustration 109

keeping those two solids stuck together, you have a better chance of getting back to the table in case you miss during your first inning.

Going back to illustration 105, if you are playing the solid balls, what would be the best approach? Once again, you should go to work right away. Your biggest problem is the cluster of two balls stuck together above ball A. Since you're in position to separate that cluster right now by playing the solid near the cluster into the corner pocket, do so immediately. Illustration 107 shows how that would look. When playing this shot, remember that the point of the shot is to make it possible to pocket the two solids that are now stuck together. If you stroke this shot too gently, you may move the balls, but still leave the lower ball of the cluster too close to the other solid for a good shot. Illustration 108 shows what could happen if you stroke this shot too softly. The solids are still tying each other up somewhat, although they are in better shape now than they were before, and both of the two balls are blocked to a degree by ball A. To avoid these problems, given the location of ball A, you will need to play the shot into the corner firmly. If you do, the result should look more like illustration 109. From here, you are much more likely to run through the rack.

Safety Play

Safety play is relatively easy in eight-ball. You will be able to apply the concepts we discussed in the straight pool and nine-ball sections of this book. In eight-ball, especially just after the rack has been broken, opportunities will abound to hide behind one or more balls in your group, leaving your opponent with no chance to shoot at the balls in his or her group. If you are playing under non-league or non-tournament conditions in a bar, however, obvious safety play should probably be avoided unless you are a lot bigger than your opponent. If winning means a great deal to you and you feel compelled to play a safety in that type of setting (even if all that is at stake is a beer), make it look like a missed shot.

• The Essentials •

1. No matter what game you are playing, go to work early by examining the table for clusters and other problems, and attacking those problems right away.

2. In straight pool, honestly evaluate your chances of making each shot. If you doubt whether you can make a particular shot, play a safety instead. In straight pool, missing any called shot is costly since every single object ball is a potential next-shot opportunity for your opponent.

3. In nine-ball, remember that you can run an entire open rack by thinking of only three balls at a time. Most critical is to make sure that you can get an angle on your next shot that will lead to your third shot.

4. In eight-ball, leave balls from your group on the table unless you are confident that you can win the game from your current position. Clearing most, but not all, of your own group of balls helps your opponents by clearing obstacles for them, and depriving yourself of shots from which you can create a pattern to get to the eight ball.

11

Practice Makes Better (If Not Perfect)

L earning to play pocket billiards well is not primarily about the quality of the teacher, but the quality of the student. A student of the game must be willing to practice, and good players distinguish themselves from the rest by their willingness to work at improving.

• Meaningful Practice •

No one improves without meaningful practice. If you examine your game for its flaws and spend the most time on those areas, you will be using your practice time in the most efficient manner possible. Your skill will improve dramatically.

When focusing on your weak points, be prepared to play worse at first. This is natural. In order to make changes in your game, you will need to stop relying on habits that may provide short-term security, but limit your ability in the long run. Also, by spending most of your time working on your weaknesses, your confidence may suffer if you lose sight of the benefits of meaningful practice. You can maintain your confidence, however, by beginning and ending your practice sessions with easier routines, even if most of your total practice time is spent on shots and exercises that will push you. Of course, when preparing for competition, the emphasis should be on raising and maintaining your confidence. In the hours before you will be playing a match, you should be warming up, not working on what you plan to improve upon.

Practicing can be either solitary or with a partner. When practicing alone, isolate one or two areas upon which you intend to focus. For example, you may want to work on your nine-ball break or safety play on a particular day. Once you've isolated an area to work on, make sure that you devote most of your practice session to that one problem area.

If you are practicing your nine-ball break, don't break and then try to run through the rack. Practice the break exclusively for at least part of your session. This means breaking, studying the results, re-racking, breaking again, and so on. Your practice sessions are your chance to experiment with different approaches or techniques that you dare not try out during a match. If you're working on your break, try adjusting your bridge, experimenting with whether you look last at the cue ball or the one ball just before you break. Test how your break changes when you stand up straighter and when you lower your break stance. Playing around with these types of adjustments during practice will give you clues on how to improve your play in the long term. Viewing yourself on videotape can also speed your progress.

Don't make pool your job. Do not force yourself to practice if there is something else you'd rather be doing (or something else you *should* be doing). Instead, take care of your priorities, and then return to pool when you are in a frame of mind to put a good effort into your game. If on any particular day you simply do not have any interest in practicing, wait until you do. Find new ways to continue to want to play and improve. Pool lore is rich with stories of all-night gambling sessions and heroically dedicated players who would practice for twelve hours at a time. Unless your dedication is such that you are considering a career in pool, however, these kinds of marathon sessions are more likely to kill your enthusiasm for pool than nurture it.

You may also find that you will succeed most quickly at pool when you are able to put it within the proper perspective, relative to other aspects of your life, and given your interest level in the game. For those of us who have already fallen in love with pool, the role of the game in our lives may be quite substantial. Even so, the difference between a game (even a fantastic and rewarding one) and more important aspects of your life should not be ignored. For others, pool is a relaxing and enjoyable pastime and nothing more. Either way, consider how much the game means to you, and then give your pool game its due in terms of how much time you devote to competing and practicing. Ironically, your game might improve with less time spent on the table . . . so long as every minute of that time is devoted willingly.

• Drills, Exercises, and Competing •

Although some players improve without ever practicing any types of drills, mixing some drills into your practice sessions can provide variety and allow you to monitor your improvement. It is important when practicing to keep your concentration level as high as possible. During practice sessions, you should push yourself to the point where competing does not seem paralyzing by contrast. If working on drills becomes tiresome, take a break from them. Going through the motions won't help you anyway, no matter how clever the drill. Wait until your interest level improves, or work on something else for awhile.

A good player goes to work right away to identify problems and figure out how to solve them. This applies to nine-ball as well as the other games. Since nine-ball is a more offense-oriented game, however, a good exercise for nine-ball is to practice running layouts with no problems. Spread out the balls and give yourself ball-in-hand on the one ball. If you miss your position or miss a shot along the way, set that shot up again. Replay each missed shot as many times as it takes until you can execute it correctly. Even if you end up replaying a number of different shots, by the time you've sunk the nine, you've successfully executed every shot necessary to run the rack. After finishing the rack, you can go back to the shots in the frame that gave you the most trouble. Keep replaying those troublesome shots until they become familiar to you.

As that drill becomes easier, give yourself tables that are not completely open. Deliberately set up clusters and force yourself to come up with a way to attack the cluster somewhere in your pattern. You can also give yourself layouts where alternate-numbered balls are on opposite ends of the table, requiring you to move the cue ball up and down the length of the table to complete the rack.

If running a full rack is beyond your current ability, start with fewer balls. Toss two balls onto the table, give yourself ball-in-hand, and pocket those two balls in sequence. When that becomes too easy, add a third ball, then a fourth . . . until you're up to a full rack.

Whether you're playing nine-ball, straight pool, or any other game, don't become obsessed with statistics. Don't dwell on running racks of balls, or 50 or 100 points of straight pool. It is better to run five balls the right way than to run twenty balls (or fifty balls, for that matter) the wrong way. Study your patterns. Are you keeping your cue ball movement to a minimum? Are you moving the cue ball to your position targets easily and without risking scratches unnecessarily? Are you playing your position without bumping into balls that can be pocketed from their original position? Are you playing the most natural position available, and avoiding the need to apply english or force the cue ball into position? Practice is the time to try two or three *different* ways to get position from one shot to the next. Experiment to find out whether alternate paths for the cue ball are superior to the one you might have picked initially.

For straight pool, spot shot drills have always been staples of my practice sessions. Start by simply trying to pocket the shot. To force yourself to pick out the point of aim each time, take your first shot from the left of the head spot, then take your next shot from the right, and alternate in that fashion for fifteen to twenty shots. Once you're comfortable sinking the spot shots, give yourself position targets and try to pocket the shot while positioning the cue ball in different areas of the table. Illustrations 110, 111, and 112 depict some targets to aim for during your spot shot drills.

In illustration 110, try to bring the cue ball two rails to the opposite side of the head spot from the starting point. You should stroke the cue ball with center and, perhaps, a touch of running english (right english in this case). Practice this shot from both sides of the table. (From the left side of the table, running english will mean left english.)

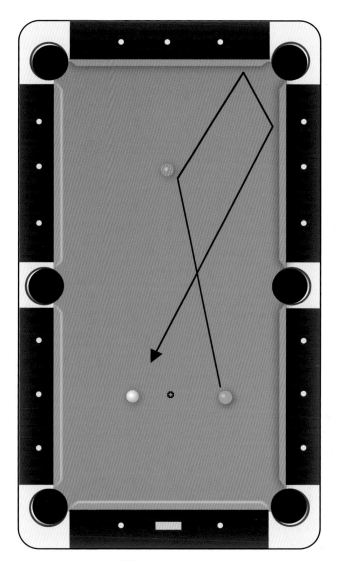

Illustration 110

In illustration 111, inside english (which is also reverse or left english in this case) will narrow the angle off the foot rail for position near the original starting point of the cue ball. Again, practice this shot from both sides of the spot.

In illustration 112, the object is to practice playing position for a ball in the shaded area at the foot of the table. This is no easy shot. A confident draw stroke is required. You may find it easier to

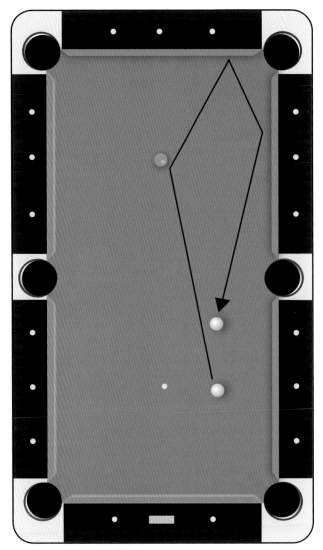

Illustration 111

execute this shot by using outside english (right english in this example). Learning to execute this shot from both sides of the table is
a valuable weapon.

    This handful of spot shot drills will help you to learn how to
move the cue ball to many different positions on the table. If you
have trouble pocketing the ball in the beginning, you can start with
an easier variation by simply moving the cue ball up but keeping
the same angle on the object ball. Whether you're starting from the

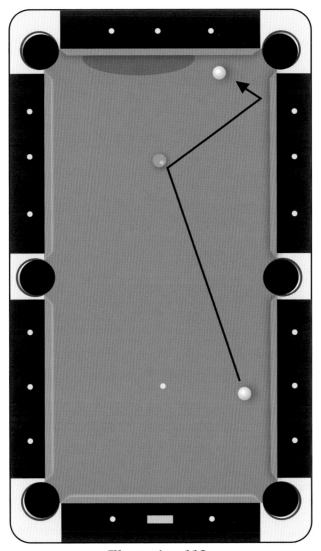

Illustration 112

head of the table or further up, work yourself up from just making the shot to pocketing the ball *and* landing the cue ball in the position target area.

There are countless drills for practicing position play. Some involve lining up object balls across the table, in a semi-circle around a pocket or in a circle around the cue ball. Illustrations 113 and 114 depict these different exercises. For the drill in illustration 113, start with the angle shown on the object ball furthest to the left, and

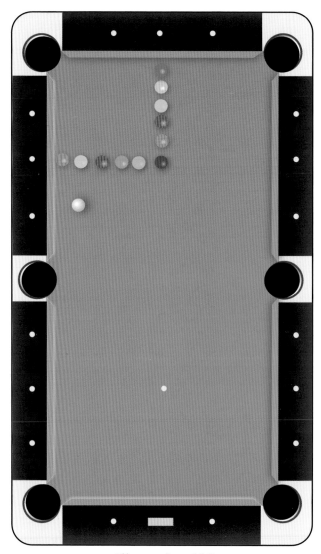

Illustration 113

try to maintain an angle on each shot so you can pocket as many of the balls in order as you can. For the drill shown in illustration 114, try to draw the cue ball back towards the center of the circle on each shot, for position on one of the remaining balls. The point of these drills is to practice controlling the cue ball. You should try drills of these type, since they teach you about your own stroke. Through repeatedly playing similar types of shots, you will develop

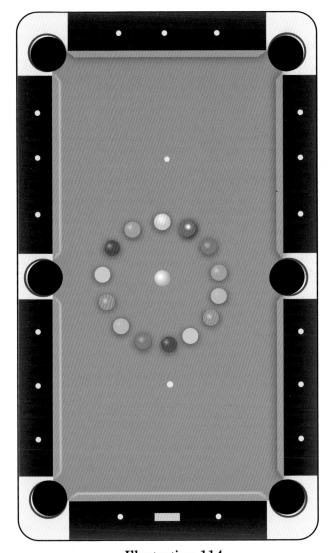

Illustration 114

a sense of how high or low you need to address the cue ball to get it to stop, draw five inches, follow two inches, and the like. You can adjust the difficulty of these drills by using less or more object balls. Since these drills are difficult, start with only a few.

Competing with another player in practice is another useful exercise, and can take several forms. You may, for example, want to compete in practice with the same intensity, rules, and etiquette that govern tournament play (no talking, ball-in-hand upon any foul, etc.). This type of practice will make competing in tournaments a more familiar, and more comfortable, experience for you. There's also great value, however, in competing less formally in practice. When doing so, you can retake a shot and try another approach if you miss your position. Also, you can ask your practice opponent why he or she played a certain pattern or applied english in a particular way. You can also get feedback from your opponent in terms of why he or she might have taken a different approach from the one you adopted. All of these benefits will be simply unavailable if you limit yourself to only practicing alone or competing in tourneys. You will improve even more quickly if you make a point of competing in practice against the widest variety of players available to you. I never enjoyed playing against slow players, but doing so taught me to be more patient.

Watching a better player is a practice exercise in itself. You can do this whether or not you are practicing against him or her. Remember that when you are lucky enough to be watching a good player, avoid merely watching the object ball. A natural tendency is to follow the moving object. Instead, look at the player's form, how her feet are aligned, how low he gets to the cue, how she bridges over a ball, how he adapts when required to stretch, how level or elevated she keeps her cue on particular shots, etc. On the subject of golf, Ben Hogan once told me, "Don't look up, you'll practically never see a good shot." This also applies to pocket billiards, whether you're the one shooting or the one watching. Don't worry about looking to see if the object ball reaches the pocket. You'll hear it if it does.

Your goal may be to enjoy pool purely socially or as a solitary pastime. Many players, including some very accomplished ones, never compete formally. For most, however, entering tournaments or competing in other ways provides an added dimension. Years ago, if a player wanted to compete, gambling was just about unavoidable. Otherwise, it was tough to get a game. Few players matched up without stakes being involved, and poolrooms did not frequently conduct tournaments or leagues for the recreational player, as is more common now. (My dad, who held weekly tournaments for all levels of players in the rooms he ran, was an exception.)

With the many leagues, ladders, and tournaments available today, competition is readily available for everyone, regardless of skill level. You will even have a choice as to the type of competition you prefer—team play versus individual competition, friendly competition versus the serious kind.

If you want to develop as a player, competition is extremely helpful. Relying on practice sessions alone is bound to improve your play, but a healthy mix of practice, instruction, and competition will bring your game along most quickly.

Competition forces you to adapt on your feet to a variety of opponents. Studying an opponent and figuring out a strategy for defeating him or her are part of playing pool. In the 1964 World Championship tourney, I came in second to Luther Lassiter. After I placed second, my wife, Ruth, told me she had never seen me take a loss so well. She was expecting me to be more disappointed and upset given the circumstances. I told her then, while eating dinner after the tournament, that I had learned enough about Lassiter to know that he was a phenomenal shot maker and an extremely tough short-game straight pool player. I also knew, however, that I would beat him if we played a long enough game. Apparently, that was accurate, since I won the title from Lassiter, 1,200–730, in a challenge match later that year. In truth, I didn't win that title just by sinking the 1,200th ball; I won it when I got Lassiter to agree to a 1,200-point match.

You will never develop your analytical skills fully through practice alone. Being forced to size up a competitor not only helps you in a match situation, it also teaches you how to study and pick apart your own game. Through the course of a game, an astute opponent will also tell you something about what parts of your game need improvement. If you tend to miss shots while shooting off the rail, you can expect an opponent to take notice and play safeties that leave you on the rail all day. The key to improvement is practicing what you don't know. In order to do that, you first have to pinpoint your weaknesses. Competition helps you, in more ways than one, to understand your weaknesses—and develop them into strengths.

• The Essentials •

1. Make your practice meaningful by focusing on your weak points.

2. Devote exclusive practice time to areas you intend to practice; for example, your safety play, your break, or shooting with the opposite hand.

3. Ask someone, an instructor if possible, to observe you at the table.

4. Combine practice and instruction with competition for the surest route towards improvement.

CHAPTER

12

Beyond This Book

s a child and teenager, I was able to study and play against players who were my idols: Ralph Greenleaf was the player I admired most, but there was also Onofrio Lauri, and Arthur Woods, a true competitor who often placed in the top three in professional tournaments, alongside of Greenleaf and Frank Taberski. I was lucky in that way since I was the son of a room owner, and I got to watch or play these players in my father's poolroom. As my game matured, I watched and played against other great players in tournaments or was booked by promoters to compete against them in exhibitions. Irving Crane, who lived in Rochester, and Joe Canton, from Troy, were not far from my home in Syracuse—all of us were living in Central New York. Having the chance to regularly watch and play against these fine players helped me immensely.

Today, you don't need to be as lucky as I was to become a good player, because so much more material is now available to help you along.

• Instruction •

Nearly all skilled musicians have taken lessons. Pianists are never ashamed to admit they've taken piano lessons. Why should it be any different for pocket billiards? Yet many good pool players are afraid to admit that they could benefit from instruction. In truth, everyone benefits from instruction.

191

To boast that you never took a lesson is to admit that you never took advantage of another way to improve. A good teacher will do more than merely give you information. He or she will also help you to analyze your mechanics and pattern play, develop routines to improve your game, and give you feedback on how you're progressing. The Billiard Congress of America (BCA) trains and certifies instructors, which can take much of the guesswork out of selecting a knowledgeable teacher. You can contact the BCA by phone at 719-264-8300, or find their web site at www.bca-pool.com.

Pool instructors today pay more attention to mechanics and form than ever before. One of the advantages of taking a lesson from a qualified instructor is that he or she can observe your mechanics and tell you what, if anything, needs to be fine-tuned or changed altogether. Just like in other sports, modern pool instruction makes use of videotape. Like hitting coaches in baseball, pool instructors today review videotape with the student and make observations concerning the player's form. (Even if you are unable to take a lesson from an instructor, there is no reason why you cannot ask a friend with a video camera to take some footage of you while you are shooting so that you at least have the chance to review your stance, your stroke preparation, and your stroke.)

Don't bother taking lessons unless you know you will have time to practice and apply what you learn. As an instructor, I was not always as patient as I wish I'd been, but I will tell you that it is frustrating to put energy into trying to teach someone the game when the student contributes barely more effort than just showing up for the lesson. If you're going to take lessons, devote yourself to practicing between lessons.

• Videotapes •

Few techniques will improve your game as surely as studying a good player. If you have the chance, you should attend as many exhibitions and pro tournaments as you can. Even if this isn't possible for you, you can study the world's best players on videotape.

The current assortment of videotapes available include recent matches between current pros, tapes of contests between past champions, instructional videotapes, trick shot collections, and more. Particularly helpful are the tapes of actual matches, which also provide commentary. These tapes give you insight into the decision making of top players. Since so much of pool depends on analyzing open racks, choosing cue ball patterns, and the like, observing and listening to professional players—on tape or live—is a wonderful source of instruction. Accu-Stats Video Productions produces and sells the biggest selection of videotaped matches. You can phone Accu-Stats at 800-828-0397, or send an e-mail to Accu-Stats@accu-stats.com.

Watching a tape of a pro just before you head to the poolroom for your weekly league match can give you a tremendous advantage. Simply watching a great player on top of his or her game will elevate your own play—even when you are not consciously studying the player. Take this "halo" effect to your next match. You'll see what I mean.

Instructional videos are of uneven quality. Unfortunately, some instructional videos are disappointing despite featuring prominent players. If you are thinking of buying an instructional video, consult with someone who's actually watched it. If that's not possible, take the time to seek out a review of the video in one of the magazines named at the end of this chapter.

• Magazines •

Billiard magazines are a great source for videotapes, equipment, and books. Two national magazines have been in print for many years, *Billiards Digest* and *Pool & Billiards*. They both publish monthly issues that contain player profiles, equipment review, instructional articles, historical pieces, and tournament schedules and results. They're also filled with advertisements for catalogs where you'll find other instructional material. Both magazines also maintain web sites. They can be found at www.billiardsdigest. com and www.poolmag.com, respectively.

While everyone will have a different aptitude for pool, it is a game where hard work and a thoughtful approach make a huge difference. Apply the principles discussed above, practice in a focused manner, and take advantage of all of the materials now available to learn more. Above all else, remember to concentrate

on the essentials of the game in practice and in the heat of competition. You will be rewarded with not only improved play, but
also a greater appreciation for perhaps the most beautiful game
ever created.

Glossary

aiming point—The point at which the center of the cue ball is aimed during a shot.

angled shot—A shot where the cue ball, object ball, and pocket are not aligned. Also called a "cut shot."

ball-in-hand—Situation where the incoming player may begin by placing the cue ball anywhere on the playing field or anywhere behind the head string (illustration 1) depending upon the rules of the particular game.

bank shot—A shot in which a ball is bounced off a cushion.

billiards (game)—General term which includes games on tables with pockets ("pool" or "pocket billiards") and games on tables without pockets (carom games); sometimes used to refer only to carom games.

break shot—The opening shot in any game. In nine-ball and eight-ball, the break is an "open break," meaning that if any object ball is pocketed, the player continues his or her inning. "Break shot" also refers to any shot where the player separates a rack or cluster of balls while pocketing a ball.

bridge—Hand formation used to support the shaft of the cue during a stroke; also used to refer to the mechanical bridge.

butt—The bottom portion of a cue. On most two-piece cues, the butt of the cue includes a wrap of linen, leather, or nylon.

call—To declare, before a shot, the ball to be pocketed and the intended pocket. Calling shots is a requirement in certain pool games, including straight pool.

carom—Any shot where a player drives the cue ball off one object ball into another object ball. Sometimes referred to as a "billiard."

195

center-ball—Stroking the cue ball without english (side-spin), follow, or draw.

combination shot—Shot in which an object ball—other than the
one initially contacted by the cue ball—is pocketed by another
object ball.

contact point—Point where the cue ball and an object ball meet.

cue ball—The white ball that is struck first on all shots in the major
pool games.

cushion—The borders of the playing field, off of which balls can be
bounced or "banked."

diamonds—Markings spaced along the rails of a table; used as reference points in pool, but more frequently in carom games.

draw—Stroke delivered by contacting the cue ball below its center
so that reverse spin is imparted to the cue ball. On straight-in
shots, draw causes the cue ball to reverse direction after contacting the object ball.

eight-ball— Game using all fifteen object balls where each player
must pocket one group of balls—either the solids (the balls
numbered one through seven) or the stripes (the balls numbered nine through fifteen)—before pocketing the eight-ball.
The winner is the player who has legally pocketed all of the
balls in his or her group, and then legally pockets the eight-
ball.

english—Side-spin applied to the cue ball by stroking the cue ball
either to the right or left of its center.

follow—Stroke delivered, in general by contacting the cue ball
above its center, so that forward spin (greater than the spin
achieved from the cue ball merely rolling naturally) is imparted to the cue ball. On straight-in shots, follow causes the
cue ball to roll forward in the same direction as the object ball.

foul—A rules infraction, which results in a penalty of some sort
such as loss of a point or the end of a player's inning. Fouls
include double-hitting the cue ball; touching the cue ball
with your body, clothing, or anything else other than the tip
of your cue; shooting while any of the balls are in motion;
shooting without keeping one or both feet touching the
floor; pushing the cue stick into the cue ball so that the tip
makes contact with the cue ball longer than for a properly
stroked shot; jumping the cue ball off the table; and jumping

the cue ball illegally (i.e., other than by striking down on the top half of the cue ball so that it springs up from the table surface).

frozen—Used to describe when a ball is touching another ball or a cushion.

full hit—Used to describe when the cue ball is stroked directly, or almost directly, into an object ball.

inning—One player's turn at the table, which continues so long as the player continues to legally pocket object balls on each shot or wins the game.

kick shot—Shot where the player banks the cue ball off a cushion prior to contacting an object ball. Also referred to as a rail-first shot. Kick shots are frequently played in nine-ball, where players often play safe by seeking to prevent their opponents from being able to contact the lowest-numbered ball on the table directly.

mechanical bridge—Device used to support the shaft of the cue on shots that require an extended reach. Consists of a bridge head (a plastic, metal, or leather piece which props up the shaft of the cue) and a stick used to steady and control the bridge head.

natural position—Positioning the cue ball for another shot using the direction in which the cue ball will tend to travel with a center-ball hit.

nine-ball—Game using the balls numbered one through nine where the player must first contact the lowest-numbered object ball on each shot. The winner of the game is the player who pockets the nine-ball on a legal shot irrespective of who has pocketed the most balls during the game.

object ball—One of the numbered balls (i.e., a ball other than the cue ball).

pattern— A planned sequence of shots.

position—The location of the cue ball as it relates to an intended shot. "Playing position" is stroking a shot so that the cue ball will stop in a location from which the next shot can be played.

rail—The wood surrounding the playing area of the table and holding the cushions in place. The term is also commonly used to refer to the cushions (e.g., "The cue ball was frozen to the rail").

safe—A legal shot where the intention is to leave an opponent without a shot; also known as a "safety." This may or may not involve pocketing an object ball.

scratch—Pocketing the cue ball.

shaft—The upper portion of a cue, including the tip. On two-piece cues, the shaft runs from the joint to the tip.

solid—Any of the object balls numbered one through seven. In the game of eight-ball, a player must pocket all of the solids or all of the stripes before attempting to win the game by pocketing the eight-ball.

straight pool—Game utilizing all fifteen object balls where the shooter may pocket any ball but must call each shot in advance. In straight pool (also known as "14.1 Continuous," or simply, "14.1"), each legally pocketed shot counts as one point, and the game is played to a predetermined total, such as 150 points.

stripe—Any of the object balls numbered nine through fifteen.

stroke—The act of striking the cue ball with the cue stick. Also refers to the motion delivered with the cue stick (comparable to a swing in baseball or golf).

tangent line—The line perpendicular to the line connecting the centers of the cue ball and an object ball at the moment the cue ball contacts the object ball. See chapter 6.

thin hit—Used to describe when the cue ball is stroked into the edge, or near the edge, of an object ball. Also called a "cut" or "thin cut."

Acknowledgments

We'd like to thank, first and foremost, our families. Thanks also to Mike Shamos and Bob Jewett for lending their expertise, counsel, and good judgment. We'd also like to thank the following friends for lending us their support: Al Conte and his sons, Victor and Al, Jr.; Rich Janosky, owner of Corky's Billiards in Syracuse, New York; George and Barbara Hadges, and Marco Macaluso of Hi-Pockets Billiards in White Plains, New York; and Greg and Ethan Hunt of Amsterdam Billiards, New York, New York. The photographs in this book were taken at Amsterdam Billiards' East Side location and at Hi-Pocket Billiards. Thank you also to Rebecca Pike and Nestle Gellerdo for appearing in photographs contained in chapter 3.

About the Authors

Arthur "Babe" Cranfield

Born on September 24, 1915, to Arthur Sr. and Isabel Cranfield, Babe lived, at various times, in the New York City borough of the Bronx; Hudson, New York, where his family operated a farm; and Syracuse, New York, where he lives today.

During much of Babe's childhood, his father owned and ran a poolroom, although its locale changed as Babe's family moved from place to place. Thus, Babe was exposed to billiards from an early age and could practice for free, advantages that combined with his natural gifts to produce an unusual talent. By the time he was 12, Babe could run 100 balls at straight pool. He also excelled as a youth in many other sports, including basketball, tennis, baseball, bowling, and golf, in which he captured a number of titles, for a while considering golf as a career.

In the 1930s Babe attended Cornell University in Ithaca, New York, intending to study agricultural techniques to benefit his family's farm. His time at college was cut short, however, when he accepted an offer to tour the country performing billiards exhibitions promoted by Sylvester Livingston, who managed tours for most of the prominent billiards stars of that era.

Babe enjoyed the distinction of being the only billiards player in history to have won the premier titles at every available level of play. In addition to many others, Babe won the United States Junior Championship when he was 15 years old; the U.S. Amateur Championship three consecutive times (in 1938, 1939, and 1940); and the World's Professional Championship in 1964. He captured the World's Professional title in a challenge match over the then–world title holder, Luther Lassiter. Contested in a multi-day "block" format, Babe prevailed by a final score of 1,200 to 730.

In recognition of his achievements, on July 19, 1997, the Billiard Congress of America inducted Babe into its Hall of Fame. Babe is also a member of the Syracuse Sports Hall of Fame.

Outside of pool, Babe made his mark by serving in the air force during World War II, and, later, joining Background Music, Inc., a major distributor for Muzak, after short stints in other jobs. Babe advanced to the position of vice president of sales within that company, where his career ultimately spanned 40 years.

In December 1940, Babe married Ruth Fish. Together they raised two sons, Lawrence and Gary, and had four grandchildren, Zachary, John, David, and Kelly. He passed away in 2004.

Laurence S. Moy

Born in 1960 in Plainfield, New Jersey, to Jack and Mary Moy, Larry grew up with his sister, Taryn, in Astoria Queens (New York), and later in Rockland County, New York. Larry first saw pocket billiards played in a poolroom next door to his parents' Chinese restaurant in Nanuet, New York. He remembers marveling at how the players he watched could somehow make the cue ball move from one end of the table to the other for position on their next shot. Larry did not start playing regularly until 1978, when he was 18 years old. That same year, he began attending Cornell University in Ithaca, where he first saw Babe Cranfield perform an exhibition.

At Cornell, Larry won the university championship and other titles numerous times. Perhaps his biggest achievement, however, was graduating with a bachelor's degree in four years (a feat many of the dedicated pool players on campus took somewhat longer to accomplish). In 1982 Larry began law school, also at Cornell, not touching a cue once in his first year of legal study but returning to the game to win the ACU-I intercollegiate title in 1985 for the region covering New York and Canada. (Although this win qualified Larry to compete in the national ACU-I tournament, no such tournament was held in 1985 due to lack of a sponsor.)

Larry now lives with his wife, Karen, and two children, Christopher and Hannah, near New York City, where he is a partner with the law firm of Liddle & Robinson, L.L.P., specializing in litigation and employment law. In addition to pool, Larry has maintained a strong interest in music (having played piano and guitar from an early age), basketball, and racquet sports (tennis, squash, and table tennis).

The highlight of Larry's pool life was being invited by the Billiard Congress of America to make the presentation for induction of Babe Cranfield into the BCA Hall of Fame in July 1997.

Index